**S**ociety **T**oday

# CHILDREN ARE PEOPLE TOO

## The Case Against Physical Punishment

Peter Newell is a writer and advocate for children's rights. From 1982 to 1988 he worked at the Children's Legal Centre in London. Previously he had been an educational journalist, helped to found an inner city alternative free school (the White Lion Street Free School), and worked at the Advisory Centre for Education.

Closely involved in the campaign against school corporal punishment, in 1972 he edited *A Last Resort? Corporal Punishment in Schools* (Penguin). In 1989 he became the first co-ordinator of EPOCH – End Physical Punishment of Children.

He lives in London and has two children, Matthew and Joe, aged four and two.

# CHILDREN ARE PEOPLE TOO

## The Case Against Physical Punishment

## Peter Newell

Bedford Square Press

Published by
BEDFORD SQUARE PRESS of the
National Council for Voluntary Organisations
26 Bedford Square, London WC1B 3HU

First published 1989

Typeset by AKM Associates (UK) Ltd, Southall, London
Printed and bound in England by
The Camelot Press, Southampton
Cover printed by Heyford Press, Wellingborough

British Library Cataloguing in Publication Data
Newell, Peter, *1940–*
    Children are people too: the case against physical punishment –
    (Society Today)
    1. Children. Rights
    I. Title   II. Series
    323.3′.52

ISBN 0-7199-1240-7

# Contents

# Acknowledgements

I would like to acknowledge, with many thanks, the help of the Trustees of the Joseph Rowntree Charitable Trust whose grant made research for this book possible.

Dr Alice Miller kindly gave me permission to quote her translation of the story of 'Little Konrad' from *For Your Own Good: The Roots of Violence in Child-Rearing* (copyright © Alice Miller, 1980, 1983; published by Virago Press, 1987).

My thanks also to Jonathan Croall, Head of Bedford Square Press, to Carole Fries for her sensitive and vital editing, and to all the others of the press who have helped with publication.

Finally, I am grateful to all the people, including the following, who have helped me by providing information and references, or by commenting on and correcting my early drafts:

In the UK, Michael Freeman, Sarah Hayes, Rachel Hodgkin, Penelope Leach, Robert Ludbrook, John and Elizabeth Newson, Nick and Lindy Peacey, Rick Rogers, Martin Rosenbaum, Tom Scott, and Ruth and Francis Seton. Also the librarians and staff of the libraries at the Institute of Psychiatry, the Institute of Child Health, the Department of Health, the National Society for the Prevention of Cruelty to Children and the National Children's Bureau.

Elsewhere, Moira Rayner, Brian Stephenson and Valerie Yule in Australia; Joav Merrick and Ole Varming in Denmark; Teuvo Peltoniemi, Heikki Sariola, Matti Savolainen and Sirpa Utriainen in Finland; Anette Engfer in Germany; Jane and James Ritchie in New Zealand; Målfrid Grude Flekkoy and Turid Vogt Grinde in Norway; Åke Edfeldt, Christina Gynna-Oguz, Sigbritt Hagbard, Lisa Hellstrom, Marianne Leni, Maria Renmyr and Tor Sverne in Sweden; Christine Hauser and Louisette Jurni-Caille in Switzerland; and Adrienne Haeuser, Dean M. Herman, Irwin A. Hyman, Adah Maurer, January H. Scott and Ralph S. Welsh in the United States.

# Preface

Hitting people is wrong – and children are people too. This book aims to help make the practice of hitting children as unacceptable in everyday life as hitting anyone else is considered to be.

It is deeply hypocritical for our society to pretend to be child-centred, to express moral outrage at the recently uncovered phenomenon of child abuse and at all other forms of criminal aggression and, at the same time, lend its support to a whole vocabulary of violence against children. Whether couched in comfortable words like 'smacking', 'spanking', 'cuffing', or stronger terms like 'beating', 'belting', 'thrashing', and 'caning', all forms of physical punishment of children entail the deliberate infliction of physical pain by one – large – person on another generally smaller, sometimes very much smaller, person. It is an unjust and bullying practice.

The support – tacit or active – we lend to it, at best causes confusion as to what level of violence *is* 'acceptable'. At worst, it leads directly to extreme abuse. All along the continuum of violence to children, from the little tap to the fatal beating, the side-effects and potential direct effects of hitting children are many. They are always undesirable: dangers to physical, psychological and sexual development; the encouragement of aggression and continuance of the cycle of violence onto others, including the next generation; links with delinquency, alcoholism, depression.

These are not exaggerated, polemical claims: they are based on research, on the findings of those who have spent most time looking at the phenomenon of violence and aggression, including family violence.

Where is the research that lends the slightest support to hitting children?

The UK has (almost) ended the use of corporal punishment in

institutions – schools, children's homes, and so on. It is time to move on quickly to end it in the family home as well. Doing so will require a great deal of public and parent education in addition to legal changes (for our legal framework currently condones, even endorses, physical punishment).

That is the purpose of a new organisation launched in 1989, EPOCH – End Physical Punishment of Children. This book is dedicated to its success – to a new epoch for children!

# Introduction

'Do that again and I'll smack you': the common refrain, heard in supermarkets, bus queues and all the other places where parenting is exposed to the public eye, causes no surprise and little if any reaction. But it could only be a child who is being addressed.

In the UK in 1989, physical punishment – smacking, slapping, spanking, hitting, beating – is not merely acceptable. Many parents regard it not just as a right, but as a duty to hit their children. The law tolerates hitting children, although hitting anyone else except in self-defence and other closely defined circumstances is a criminal offence.

This book sets out to change the attitudes to children which underlie their day-to-day experience of violence at the hands of parents and other carers. The purpose is not to make parents feel guilty, but to persuade everyone at last to accept the fundamental injustice of a very common practice which is also dangerous in a variety of ways. Many parents already agree that hitting children is ineffective and there is ample research evidence to support them (see page 16). While social pressures to use physical punishment remain so strong, parents can hardly be blamed for fulfilling the social norm. But a sizeable minority have already resolved not to hit their children (as have the overwhelming majority in some other countries – see page 67). Just as children need limits, so child-rearing adults need limits, and once these are defined to include a ban on hitting children, it is easier to be consistent and to develop positive alternatives.

This book does not pretend to provide a manual of good parenting, listing practical alternatives to hitting children, as much material already exists (see Appendix 2).

Being hit by their parents (frequently, and often with implements) is not the only ill suffered by children. Our society remains divided by basic inequalities: by poverty, homelessness, unemployment and by discrimination on grounds of disability, race and sex. Far from challenging these, current policies in many ways exacerbate them. Parenthood – and this still largely means motherhood – remains under stress, often extreme stress. In her book *Of Woman Born*, Adrienne Rich analyses the oppression of women and children by 'the institution of motherhood'. She argues that the impossible demands of the institution, coupled with a social (patriarchal) devaluation of motherhood, leads to both rage and guilt in mothers. Children, no matter how well loved, are often the nearest targets of their mothers' frustration. Rich writes that the institution of motherhood must be destroyed: 'To destroy the institution is not to abolish motherhood. It is to release the creation and sustenance of life into the same realm of decision, struggle, surprise, imagination and conscious intelligence, as any other difficult, but freely chosen work.'[1]

Childhood, too, is an institution. Society, even in those areas like education which are supposedly for the benefit of children, remains unsympathetic to them. All too often children are treated as objects, with no provision made for hearing their views or recognising them as fellow human beings. Children – seen but not heard – face the double jeopardy of discrimination on grounds of age, and discrimination on all the other grounds as well. Giving legal sanction to hitting children confirms and reflects their low status.

Some, while supporting the principle that children should not be hit, argue that the priority must be to confront the basic inequalities, that it is unfair on families and parents, and will compound their problems, to seek to end such a common, 'normal' practice. They go on to argue that 'criminalising' physical punishment through legal changes would lead to more policing of the families already most policed, more state intervention and more children being taken unwillingly away from their families into state care.

This view is based on many misconceptions. Stopping hitting children does not compound problems, it starts to solve them. Hitting is not the prerogative of 'poor' parents, or of certain classes or cultures (the largest survey of child-rearing practices in the UK, for example, found more parents in social classes I and II admitting to using an implement to discipline their 7-year-old child; see page 56).

But, above all, the view perpetuates a fundamental injustice. Why should children alone wait for equal protection from violence, while we seek to correct all the other social wrongs? Ending the socially condoned hitting of children is a necessary – but, of course, not sufficient – condition for improving their status in society.

The legal changes that are needed to prohibit physical punishment, which this book argues for, would not create a new criminal offence. These changes are not about punishing parents. They are about changing attitudes to children by removing the current acceptance and endorsement of physical punishment. They are to provide a context and a basis for education. To remove the current injustice, parents must lose their common law rights to use physical punishment. There should be a clear statement to that effect in children's law. Technically a parent who smacked a child could then be prosecuted under the law on assault (parents can already be prosecuted for punishment which is not 'moderate and reasonable'). This would provide an essential equity: children would have no less and no more protection from assault than other people.

Technically, the lightest of touches amounts to an assault which could lead to prosecution. But relatives and friends do not seek to have each other prosecuted for minor or occasional assaults – unless they are deeply aggrieved by them; if they are, it is surely right that they should have a legal remedy. Is anyone arguing for a return to legally sanctioned wife- or servant-beating? In any case, unless the assault is serious and there are adult witnesses and medical evidence, there will be obvious problems over pursuing the prosecution.

Another misconception is that a ban on physical punishment would inhibit parents and others from taking action to protect a child from danger – such as, grabbing the child who is running into a busy road, or approaching the hot oven. But there is a clear line between the infliction of pain as a punishment, and physical action to avert danger. This is defined, for example, in the law which now prevents teachers using corporal punishment, but allows them to take action to protect pupils and others.[2]

It is 10 years since Sweden adopted a ban on physical punishment as part of its family law (see page 70). In that time, there have been criminal prosecutions for serious child abuse. But only one parent has been prosecuted for 'mild' physical punishment: following a report by his son, a father was fined the equivalent of £9. There have, as yet, been no similar cases in the other countries which have banned physical punishment. The purpose and the effect of the changes in these countries have been to change attitudes.

And, of course, it is not in the interests of children to give the state new powers to remove them unwillingly from their parents. That is not the purpose in 'banning' physical punishment, nor should it be an unintended consequence. The current Children Bill only permits children to be taken into care against their parents' wishes under very strict conditions. The fact that a child has been physically punished, even if this becomes unlawful, would not by itself lead to a care order.[3]

There is no reason to believe that a legal prohibition will increase state intervention in families. In the Scandinavian countries the level of intervention is, in any case, lower than in the UK, and decreasing steadily (see page 86). By heightening awareness of the injustice of hitting children, and removing confusion about 'acceptable' levels of violence, legal reforms accompanied by education campaigns are likely to reduce the kinds of abuse that make intervention, on occasion, essential.

But it should be clear that the case against physical punishment is not based primarily on obvious connections with serious child abuse, strong though the evidence is. The basic argument is that children are people, and hitting people is wrong. That hitting children is, in addition, ineffective and carries with it all kinds of immediate and delayed dangers makes action long overdue.

## Historical Attitudes to Children

The history of childhood is a nightmare from which we have only recently begun to awaken. The further back in history one goes, the lower the level of child care, and the more likely children are to be killed, abandoned, beaten, terrorized and sexually abused . . . That this pattern has not previously been noted by historians is because serious history has long been considered a record of public not private events. Historians have concentrated so much on the noisy sandbox of history, with its fantastic castles and magnificent battles, that they have generally ignored what is going on in the homes around the playground. And where historians usually look to the sandbox battles of yesterday for the causes of those today, we instead ask how each generation of parents and children creates those issues which are later acted out in the arena of public life.

Thus Lloyd deMause begins his classic *History of Childhood*.[4]

The book provides a gruelling overview of the 'nightmare' of infanticide, abandonment, beating and sexual abuse through the centuries. deMause documents, for example, that

. . . contrary to the usual assumption that it is an Eastern rather than a Western problem, infanticide of both legitimate and illegitimate children was a regular practice of antiquity, that the killing of legitimate children was only slowly reduced during the middle ages (hence the grossly unequal ratios of men to women in many societies), and that illegitimate children continued to be regularly killed right up into the nineteenth century . . . Even though Thomas Coram opened his Foundling Hospital in 1741 because he couldn't bear to see the dying babies lying in the gutters and rotting in the dung-heaps of London, by the 1890s dead babies were still a common sight in London streets . . . Urges to mutilate, burn, freeze, drown, shake and throw the infant violently about were continuously acted out in the past.

deMause also describes formal and informal abandonment of children, as well as their imprisonment, through swaddling and other physical restraints.

The evidence deMause has collected leads him to believe that 'a very large percentage of the children born prior to the eighteenth century were what would today be termed "battered children" '. His search through 200 statements of advice on child-rearing found that most approved of beating children severely, and all allowed beating to some degree except three – Plutarch, Palmieri and Sadoleto. 'The beatings described in the sources were generally severe, involved bruising and bloodying of the body, began early, and were a regular part of the child's life.' Thus 'century after century of battered children grew up and in turn battered their own children. Public protest was rare. Even humanists and teachers who had a reputation for great kindness, like Petrarch, Ascham, Comenius and Pestalozzi approved of beating children.'

deMause does believe that things have improved over the centuries: 'Some attempts were made in the seventeenth century to limit the beating of children, but it was the eighteenth century which saw the biggest decrease. The earliest lives I have found of children who may not have been beaten at all date from 1690 to 1750.' But in Copenhagen in 1748, death statistics reveal that of the 3,328 who died, 987 died because of hitting and beating: the clerk recording the statistics noted that most of them were children.[5] Certain states of America still had 'stubborn child laws', prescribing the death penalty for children who disobeyed their parents, in the seventeenth century.[6]

He has found it more difficult to research the history of sexual abuse, as 'the bulk of books relating to sex in history remain under lock and key in library storerooms and museum basements all over Europe, unavailable even to the historian'. But he adds that there is evidence enough to indicate that sexual abuse was 'far more common in the past than today'. (deMause was writing in the mid-1970s, before the current explosion of interest and concern at sexual abuse; he might review this conclusion today.)

Dr Alice Miller, whose books[7] challenging violent child-rearing as the root of violence and cruelty in society have received world-wide recognition, looked at German child-rearing manuals of the eighteenth and nineteenth centuries. She quotes J. Sulzer, writing in 1748:

> If willfulness and wickedness are not driven out, it is impossible to give a child a good education . . . I advise all those whose concern is the education of children to make it their main occupation to drive out willfulness and wickedness and to persist until they have reached their goal . . . if parents are fortunate to drive out willfulness from the very beginning by means of scolding and the rod, they will have obedient, docile and good children . . .
>
> Over the years, children forget everything that happened to them in early childhood. If their wills can be broken at this time, they will never remember afterwards that they had a will, and for this very reason the severity that is required will not have any serious consequences.

Alice Miller quotes one moral tale from another German child-rearing guide at the end of the eighteenth century which illustrates several of the classic clichés of physical punishment: 'spare the rod and spoil the child', 'it hurts me more than it hurts you', etc. 'Little Konrad's father' had made a firm resolve not to hit his son.

> 'But it didn't turn out as I had hoped. An occasion soon arose when I was compelled to use the rod . . . Cristel came to visit and brought a doll. No sooner had Konrad seen it than he wanted to have it. I asked Cristel to give it to him, and she did. After Konrad had held it for a while, Cristel wanted it back, and Konrad didn't want to give it to her. What was I to do now? If I had brought him his picture book and then said he should give the doll to Cristel, perhaps he would have done it without objecting. But I didn't think of it, and even if I had, I don't know whether I would have done it. I thought it was high time for the child to accustom himself to obeying his father unquestioningly. I therefore said: "Konrad, don't you want to give Cristel's doll back to her?"

"No!" he said with considerable vehemence.

"But poor Cristel has no doll!"

"No!" he answered again, started to cry, clutched the doll and turned his back on me.

Then I said to him in a severe tone of voice: "Konrad, you must return the doll to Cristel at once, I insist."

And what did Konrad do? He threw the doll at Cristel's feet. Heavens, how upset I was by this. If my best cow had died, I don't think I would have been as shocked. Cristel was about to pick up the doll, but I stopped her. "Konrad", I said, "pick the doll up at once and hand it to Cristel."

"No! No!" cried Konrad.

Then I fetched the switch, showed it to him and said: "Pick up the doll or I will have to give you a whipping." But the child remained obstinate and cried, "No! No!".

Then I raised the switch and was about to strike him when a new element was added to the scene. His mother cried, "Dear husband, I beg you, for heaven's sake –"

Now I was faced with a dilemma. I made a quick resolve, however, took the doll and the switch, picked up Konrad, ran out of the room and into another, locked the door behind me so his mother could not follow, threw the doll on the ground and said: "Pick up the doll or I will give you a whipping!" My Konrad persisted in saying no.

Then I lashed him, one! two! three! "Don't you want to pick up the doll now?" I asked.

"No!" was his reply.

Then I whipped him much harder and said: "Pick up the doll at once!"

Then he finally picked it up; I took him by the hand, led him back into the other room and said: "Give the doll to Cristel."

He gave it to her.

Then he ran crying to his mother and wanted to put his head in her lap. But she had enough sense to push him away and said: "Go away, you're not my good Konrad."

To be sure, the tears were rolling down her cheeks as she said it. When I noticed this, I asked her to leave the room . . .

I can certainly say that my heart was sore throughout this scene, partly because I felt pity for the child, partly because I was distressed by his stubbornness.

At mealtime I could not eat; I got up from the table and went to see our pastor and poured my heart out to him. I was comforted by what he said: "You did the right thing, dear Mr Kiefer", he said. "When the nettles are still young, they can be pulled out easily; but if they are left for a long time, the roots will grow, and then if one attempts to pull them out, the roots will be deeply embedded. It is the same way with misbehaviour in children. The longer one overlooks it, the more difficult it is to eliminate. It was also a good thing for you to give the stubborn little fellow a thorough whipping. He won't forget it for a long time to come . . ." "[8]

Perhaps one should feel relieved that Konrad's father could at least conceive that an alternative strategy – finding Konrad's picture book – might have avoided all the violence and the humiliation.

The purpose of this cursory look at the history of childhood is to indicate some of the background to current assumptions in this and other cultures that it is a right or a duty to hit children. (Those who seek psychoanalytical explanations of why children are hit should read more of deMause and Alice Miller.) That we have 'begun to awaken' from the nightmare is obvious, and indeed an understatement of the progress that has been made. But much of that progress has been a struggle, and most of it has been very recent. The 'discovery' of child cruelty only happened at the end of the last century. While legislation to protect animals from cruelty dates from 1823, it was 1889 before legislation on cruelty to children was enacted – the Prevention of Cruelty to and Protection of Children Act.

Samuel Radbill, in his article, 'A History of Child Abuse and Infanticide', tells the story of the founding of the first Society for the Prevention of Cruelty to Children, in New York. It followed an incident in which some church workers tried to get action taken to prevent maltreatment of a child called Mary Ellen, who was being beaten regularly and was malnourished by her parents. There was no law under which any agency could interfere on her behalf. The workers appealed to the Society for the Prevention of Cruelty to Animals, which promptly took action: 'They were able to have Mary Ellen removed from her parents on the grounds that she was a member of the animal kingdom and that therefore her case could be included under the laws against animal cruelty.'[9]

The concept of 'child battering' is even more recent: in the 1940s and 1950s the use of X-rays led to revelations of deliberately inflicted injuries; and, in the early sixties, an American paediatrician, Dr Henry Kempe, became alarmed at the number of children admitted to hospitals suffering from non-accidental injury. In 1961 the American Academy of Pediatrics held a symposium on child abuse under Dr Kempe's direction, and to emphasise the seriousness of the problem, he proposed the term 'the battered child syndrome'.

But the 'discovery' of child abuse certainly did not mark the end, or even the beginning of the end, of physical punishment of children in British and other cultures. The gradual elimination of corporal punishment of adults in the UK began in the last century. Flogging in the army was abolished in 1906; birching as judicial punishment was ended (except in the Isle of Man) in 1948; flogging in the navy was banned in 1957. Then corporal punishment in prisons and borstals ended in 1967. It took another 20 years of hard campaigning (see Chapter 5), however, to ban beating in state-supported education – abolition finally taking effect on 15 August 1987. Even then the government insisted that parents should be allowed to pay for the privilege of having their children beaten in independent schools. Once the promised ban on physical punishment in all child care institutions is in effect, probably by the end of 1989 (see page 108), the private schools will be the only UK institutions to tolerate the hitting of children.

It appears that the only official body in the UK which has so far advocated the end of all physical punishment of children was the government-appointed Children's Committee, in 1981. This was also, perhaps coincidentally, the year of its untimely death. The multidisciplinary committee appointed by ministers was set up just two years earlier in 1979 to advise the government and all concerned on the needs of children. In one of its final reports, the committee promoted its 'convinced and unanimous' opinion that corporal punishment was wrong, and recommended: 'The United Kingdom should embark upon a progressive programme, governed by a specific timescale, to eliminate the use of corporal punishment on children and young people.'[10]

By then, in 1979, Sweden had become the first country specifically to ban physical punishment (see page 70). Less publicised, Switzerland had removed the confirmation of parents' right to hit children from its federal law the previous year (see page 68). Finland (1984), Denmark (1986) and Norway (1987) quickly followed Sweden's lead. Then, in March 1989, Austria became the fifth country in Europe to ban hitting children (see page 68). In 1985 the Council of Europe Committee of Ministers (including our own Foreign Secretary), considering action against violence in the family, recommended that member states, including the UK, should 'review their legislation on the power to punish children in order to limit or indeed prohibit corporal punishment, even if violation of such a prohibition does not necessarily entail a criminal penalty'.[11]

In October 1988, the Children's Legal Centre's magazine, *Childright*, carried an article by a prominent law professor advocating legislation to end parents' rights to hit their children: 'If we are to assert the dignity of all persons, to affirm equal respect for all persons, we must as a necessary pre-condition protect the bodily integrity of all. If we are concerned to eliminate the evil of child abuse, we must ultimately accept that corporal punishment of children is child abuse.' There was massive publicity on television, radio and in the newspapers, but the proposal was treated with seriousness and little tabloid hysteria. (The author, Professor Michael Freeman, in common with other 'stop smacking' advocates, did, however, receive some very abusive mail.)[12]

This was a sign of the times. For 1988 was also the year in which the report into child abuse in Cleveland had prefaced its recommendations on children with the phrase: 'The child is a person, not an object of concern.'[13] It was the year in which the Children Bill was presented to Parliament – a Bill which in many ways improves the status of the child, the rights of children to have a voice, and even increasingly to make decisions for themselves. Several of the largest child welfare organisations, including Barnardo's and the Children's Society, decided it was time to re-vamp their own projections of childhood, to replace grim images of oppression with 'happy smiling faces' – new autonomous figures to promote the child's voice and child-centred policies. 'A breakthrough for children's rights', trumpeted the fiftieth issue of *Childright* in September 1988.

Given this mood of change, it was no surprise that while the Children Bill was in the House of Lords in January 1989, parents' rights to hit children should come under parliamentary scrutiny for the first time since the end of the last century. They were only tentatively challenged: an attempt was made to remove the statutory endorsement of parents' punishment rights in the legislation which otherwise prohibits cruelty, but without removing their common law rights to use 'moderate and reasonable' punishment. The House of Lords did come near to removing foster parents' rights to hit children – but even this reform was lost by 19 votes. Some attitudes showed that we are not yet out of the nightmare. One peer, ironically a member of the Central Executive Committee of the National Society for the Prevention of Cruelty to Children, hoped that others 'will feel there is a place for beating – I shall not call it corporal punishment – in family life'.[14]

The new United Nations Convention on the Rights of the Child, which will hopefully be finalised during 1989, is sadly silent on the specific issue of physical punishment, but it does insist that

> States Parties shall take all appropriate legislative, administrative, social and educational measures to protect the child from *all forms* of physical or mental violence, injury or abuse, neglect or negligent treatment, maltreatment or exploitation including sexual abuse, while in the care of parent(s) legal guardian(s) or any other person who has the care of the child. [15]

If the UK is to ratify the Convention (and it will be internationally humiliating if we do not), there will surely have to be action on physical punishment.

The emergence in April 1989 of a new organisation, EPOCH – End Physical Punishment of Children, which aims to end physical punishment through public and parent education, information, research and legal reforms, will hopefully provide a focus to finally challenge the acceptability of hitting children. We were the last country in Europe to end (or almost end) school beating. We do not have to be the last to renounce physical punishment altogether. World-wide, the UK bears a heavy responsibility for promoting violence to children, as many countries where school beating still continues were once part of the British Empire. There is still an opportunity to make some amends.

# CHAPTER 1

## WHAT'S WRONG WITH HITTING CHILDREN?

*'It is very noticeable that parents who injure their children, at whatever age and however seriously, more often than not relate the event to a concept of punishment, even when they accept that they went "too far".'*
(David Jones and others, *Understanding Child Abuse*, 1987)

### The Basic Injustice

There is an injustice and illogicality in suggesting that it is acceptable to hit children, but that it is quite unacceptable for them to hit others, or for adults to hit anyone else. Hitting people is wrong – and children are people too.

The inescapable conclusion is that the widespread use of hitting, smacking, slapping and beating in child-rearing today, both in the UK and much of the rest of the world, is based on an historical attitude which sees children as less than people.

Our language has developed a remarkable vocabulary to cover hitting children – smacking, slapping, spanking, slippering, paddling, clouting, cuffing, boxing and clipping the ears, rapping the knuckles, beating, caning (six of 'the best'), tawsing, thrashing, belting, strapping, giving a good hiding, tanning, walloping, whacking. Even the softer, more comfortable words like smacking and spanking conceal the deliberate infliction of physical pain of varying degrees. In addition to the physical pain, the circumstances are generally humiliating and degrading to the child.

A fundamental implication of treating children as people is that they should have equal protection from all forms of violence. As a member of the European Commission of Human Rights argued in an early report concerning school corporal punishment: 'Corporal punishment amounts to a total lack of respect for the human being; it therefore cannot depend on the age of the human being.'[1] In Sweden and Finland, two of the Scandinavian countries which have prohibited all forms of physical punishment of children (see Chapter 3, page 67), an emphasis on 'children as people' has led to principles in family law emphasising individuality and children's own views. The Finnish Child Custody and Right of Access Act 1983 states that the objects of custody 'are to ensure the well-being and the well-balanced development of a child according to his individual needs and wishes'. Before making decisions about a child's life, parents and other custodians must 'where possible discuss the matter with the child taking into account the child's age and maturity and the nature of the matter. In making the decision the custodian shall give due consideration to the child's feelings, opinions and wishes.'[2] The Swedish Parenthood and Guardianship Code (revised in 1983) insists that 'children are to be treated with respect for their person and individuality'.[3] An official from the Swedish Ministry of Justice, explaining the thinking behind the new law, said: 'By the prohibition of physical punishment, the legislator wanted to show that a child is an independent individual who can demand full respect for his or her person, and who should thus have the same protection against physical punishment or violence as we adults see as being totally natural for ourselves.' A pamphlet from the ministry emphasises that 'our democratic community needs children taught to think for themselves, who are used to making their own choices and to shouldering responsibility. It is impossible to beat a child into obedience and at the same time expect it to be able to think for itself' (see pages 75 and 77).

One measure of how society regards groups within it is the comparative degree of protection afforded to them. Over the years in the UK there has been a growing but gradual acceptance of the wrongness, and also of the ineffectiveness and dangers, of hitting people as punishment. Thus our society has moved away from treating as acceptable the hitting of wives, servants and apprentices; more recently, away from acceptance of corporal punishment in the armed forces and judicial corporal punishment; and, most recently, away from allowing children to be hit in schools and child care institutions.

But the injustice and the weight of evidence against the practice does not stop short at the front door of the family home. When it comes to children, our law positively endorses 'moderate and reasonable' chastisement (see Chapter 4, page 97). Until protection is fully extended to them, we continue to confirm their low status.

An American sociologist, William J. Goode, looking at the use of force in family life, concluded that the amount of it was 'neither necessary or desirable'. He sees injustice as the root cause of force, in the family as in the wider society:

> It is not only possible but we think likely, that some part of every social system is pervaded by force only because some or many of its participants believe the system is unjust; therefore, those who dominate must use force to maintain it.
>
> Women, children, slaves, colonials, lower castes and other disadvantaged segments of any society are constrained more than others by force . . .
>
> However, as the worldwide revolutionary temper of our era amply shows, when the disadvantaged learn how much of the social structure is not embedded unchangeably in the cosmos but is held in place by force wielded by human beings, they become less willing to comply with its traditional rules. Perhaps one could even say . . . that we could test whether and where justice is to be found, by removing more and more physical force as a support. The system which needs least support of this kind would, I think, be a closer approximation of justice than any we know now.[4]

The Bible – or, perhaps even more so, later misrepresentations of what the Bible says – has played a prominent part in promoting the beating of children. 'Spare the rod and spoil the child' has its roots in Proverbs 13:24: 'He that spareth his rod hateth his son; but he that loveth him chasteneth him betimes.' Two Americans much involved in the campaign to end school beating have produced a pamphlet carefully analysing this and other biblical references. They conclude: 'There is no authority in the Bible for the corporal punishment of children with rod or otherwise, except in the Proverbs of Solomon. It is only Solomon who recommends child-beating. Never the Lord.' They also find contrary advice from Jesus, Apostle John and Paul.[5] The established churches in the UK eventually found no difficulty in condemning school beating in unequivocal terms, and in Scandinavia they have supported the prohibition of parental physical punishment too. There are still small sects who preach the pernicious and discredited doctrine of original sin and the need to beat it out of children. Rational arguments about children's rights to justice and protection are unlikely to make much impact on them.

The substantial body of research on immediate and later effects and side-effects of physical punishment, summarised in this chapter, demonstrates the ineffectiveness, and also the dangers involved, beyond the basic injustice. A search through many of London's largest specialist libraries has failed to find any studies at all which actually promote physical punishment as a useful tool with beneficial outcomes. There are many studies, however, demonstrating that the use of rational explanations for desired behaviour with children, the use of affection, praise and encouragment to reinforce desired behaviour, and appeals to the child's pride tend to produce children with highly developed levels of self-control and highly developed moral standards.

A danger of highlighting the research findings which argue against hitting children is that it may divert attention from the fundamental injustice – the lack of respect for children as people. The research may even suggest that if it 'worked', and had no obvious side-effects, it would be a respectable practice. But reciting the evidence may convince some who cannot yet concede (probably because of their own childhoods) that children should have equal protection from the deliberate infliction of physical pain.

People sometimes respond to research findings which link the use of physical punishment to later aggression, delinquency, alcoholism, depression and practically every other undesirable condition by saying 'but I was smacked/spanked/beaten regularly as a child and it never did me any harm'. For example, whenever the issue of corporal punishment is raised in the House of Lords, there are always several peers who preface their remarks with some statement along these lines. During an unsuccessful attempt to push through legislation abolishing school beating in 1973, Lord Platt became impatient with hearing the above phrase: 'I think that is about the most egotistic statement that any person could make. My answer to it is: "My dear old fellow, you don't realise what harm it did." The development of the stiff upper lip is liable to be accompanied by the development of a similarly rigid mind.'[6]

Reviewing the evidence on the side-effects of hitting children, New Zealand researchers Jane and James Ritchie emphasise in their book *Spare the Rod* that the conclusions of psychological studies are about probabilities, not about every individual case:

> The generalisations of psychological research can indicate a likelihood or probability. Thus, reading these research conclusions, an individual may well say, 'My mother hit me and I'm not aggressive' or 'My father hit me and I'm all right', and that may

be perfectly true for the individual. But that is not the point. We are talking here about trends, probabilities and social policy, not about particular individuals and their case histories.[7]

One very clear conclusion of research is that people's own childhood experience – whether or not their parents hit them – heavily influences their later attitudes to the use of physical punishment. A Swedish opinion poll in 1981 revealed that 41 per cent of those who had been physically punished believed that it was necessary to use it in bringing up children, compared with only 11 per cent of those who had not been hit by their parents. Eighty-six per cent of those who had not received physical punishment, compared with 56 per cent of those who had, believed parents should manage without it (see page 81).

A survey of the mass of international research findings may have the undesirable effect of suggesting new comparative studies. Action rather than more research is now needed; surely the dangers have been sufficiently exposed. There may have to be research into the current prevalence of physical punishment and attitudes to its use in the UK, to convince parliamentarians and others that action is urgently needed. Even if we were dealing with some 'neutral' practice, surely the arguments against it have been overwhelmingly made? But the legalised hitting of children is not 'neutral': it reflects a fundamental injustice.


## It Doesn't Even Work

Very young children who are not able to understand language will be unable to understand why they are being hit (or indeed if the hitting has any connection with their behaviour). At the same time, psychoanalysts have suggested that the pain that a very young child feels when being beaten is a good deal more intense than an adult would feel. The child has not learnt to differentiate time, and so is unable to anticipate that the current sensations will come to an end: every experience has a 'timeless' and therefore more intense quality.

But despite the obvious ineffectiveness and the probably heightened pain, research suggests that almost two-thirds of British parents smack their under 1-year-old child (see page 54). Penelope Leach's classic practical handbook, *Baby and Child* – which in common with many, but unfortunately not all, current child-rearing manuals takes a strong stand against hitting – tells parents of babies aged under 1:

If you actually punish him physically, shaking him, smacking him or dumping him in his cot, he will be as amazed and horrified as you would be if the family dog suddenly turned on you and took a chunk out of your leg. Whatever you do to him in anger, he will not understand why . . . Research has shown that smacked children can never remember what they were smacked *for*. Pain and indignity make them so angry that they go away seething with anger rather than full of repentance.[8]

Miriam Stoppard repeats the same message in her *Baby Care Book*: 'Corporal punishment will only lead to problems. I think it should be avoided at all costs. In any case research has shown that children don't know what they are being smacked for. They cannot remember, so they don't associate the punishment with the crime, and smacking doesn't act as a deterrent.'[9]

A report in *Developmental Psychology* in 1986 described interviews about methods of discipline with mothers of 1-year-old babies at a clinic at the University of Houston. It revealed that the babies punished physically were the least likely to obey instructions not to touch breakables, and, perhaps more significantly, that seven months later the physically punished children lagged behind the others in developmental tests.[10]

The early behavioural psychologists – J. B. Watson and B. F. Skinner – rejected physical punishment. Watson suggested that the punishment would either be too rare or mild to establish a conditioned negative response, or too frequent, leading to habituation and possibly masochism[11] (see page 48). More recently, some psychologists have argued that physical punishment can be effective to some degree – but only under carefully controlled conditions. As one noted, contrary to these requirements for punishment 'effectiveness', parental physical punishment is typically 'ill-timed, erratic and administered vengefully'.[12] The sort of conditions which must be carefully regulated if punishment is to be effective include the type of punishment, the time-lag between its infliction and the undesired behaviour, its duration and the availability of alternative behaviours. The intensity of the punishment must also be scientifically controlled and be at as high a degree as practicable. It is only under those sorts of conditions that psychologists have reported any substantial degree of success in eliminating undesired behaviour through physical punishment.

Writing in *Four Years Old in an Urban Community*, John and

Elizabeth Newson (whose research on the prevalence of physical punishment in the UK is summarised in Chapter 3, page 50) say:

> Those mothers who think that smacking has any functional role in learning invariably talk about the results it will have in the *future*, whether immediate, short-term or long-term; whereas the act of smacking invariably occurs as the culminating point of a sequence of events, and therefore has its roots in the immediate past. This in effect means that punishment in the context of mother/child conflict differs in two very basic ways from the experimental learning situation of the laboratory . . .
>
> Not only does punishment in the family context involve social interaction of a very intimate and emotive kind; it also comes about after a series of behavioural events in which the child is an equal participant, and during which he is given the opportunity of becoming aware of his own role as provoker of punishment and of his mother's intention to punish if he continues in it . . . To regard smacking as an ordinary example of avoidance conditioning, rather than as one part of a complicated communicational pattern between mother and child, is to simplify it out of all recognition; not least because, while a laboratory experiment can continue the process until learning occurs, the mother in practice is restricted in her behaviour, both by the individual reaction of the child . . . and by her own conscience.[13]

An American clinical psychologist who has researched and written extensively on the effects of violence in childhood, Norma D. Feshbach of the University of California, Los Angeles, writes:

> Punishment not only fails to communicate to the child what is the desired response but its effect even as a suppressor depends on the right combination of a complex set of parameters including timing, intensity, consistency and the affectional relationship between the child and the punitive agent . . . It is also of note that experimental studies on punishment have been primarily concerned with the impact of punishment on the undesired response, and rarely assessed possible incidental consequences of punishment such as anxiety and hostility. There is a considerable amount of research which indicates that physical pain strongly elicits aggressive behaviour as well as producing fears of the painful situation and of generalized stimuli that are difficult to extinguish . . . If we combine the

experimental research on punishment with the data on the effects of physical pain, it would appear that physical punishment has limited utility as a response suppressor and may well produce incidental effects with negative consequences for the child's adjustment that can be more undesirable than the response being punished.[14]

This kind of research can raise ethical issues. An American lawyer, Dean M. Herman, who has reviewed much of the research evidence, writing in the American journal, *Family Law Quarterly*, reflects his shock at the behaviour of some of the psychologists. It

... gives us an idea of how dangerously detached we can get from the effects of physical punishment on others. For example, one psychologist coolly notes the 'strong . . . avoidance behaviour' that a six year-old girl demonstrated on being subjected to shocks . . . Another psychologist, who administered 500-volt shocks to a child with a cattle prod, wrote that his subject's reactions to the shocks 'may be of interest'. 'The first shock elicited a scream', and when subsequent shocks were 'due', 'Mike ran to a corner of the room, jumped in place, hit himself and yelled'.

Dean Herman comments: 'Psychologists today conducting studies in behaviour control prefer to use electric shocks, which have a deceptively innocuous connotation, rather than beatings and whippings on their subjects.'[15]

A series of studies have shown that an individual's response to physical punishment is limited to the particular situation: even if a smack immediately stops a child doing something, which it will certainly do on occasion, the alteration in behaviour will only apply to that situation and not to other behaviour which leads to verbal prohibition or warnings. Moreover, the modification in the child's behaviour is likely to last only as long as there is a high probability that engaging in it will lead to more physical punishment.[16]

In New Zealand, Jane and James Ritchie, who surveyed punishment rates in the sixties and seventies, indicate that only 14 per cent of their 1977 sample of mothers found physical punishment 'unequivocally effective', compared with 41 per cent of their 1963 sample. But the 1977 group were using it more frequently. The Ritchies comment in *Spare the Rod*: 'Why on earth do they, then, continue to do it if most think it ineffective? A finding like this is a clear indicator that one is not dealing with a pragmatic, rational world but with a deeply entrenched belief system relatively impervious to change, and widely supported in other parts of society and by the ideology of punishment.'[17]

The Ritchies are among the very few researchers who have asked children – a sample of 12- and 13-year-olds – how they feel about being hit by parents: 'Most of the children do not think smacking does any good. It occurs within a family context where they know and can expect it will occur in certain ways, but apparently they continue to behave in those ways, in spite of the likelihood of punishment . . . Overall our data shows that both parents and 12 and 13 year-olds agree that physical punishment is an ineffective way of changing behaviour.' The Ritchies also report that 'in one quarter of the sample these children are hit hard enough for it to hurt. They also want to hit back but dare not. Only a tiny percentage feel sorry (7 per cent of the boys, 16 per cent of the girls). Maybe when they were little they could accept the pain and hurt and humiliation with bafflement or as a matter of daily fact, but not at 12 or 13. Now resentments will simmer, grudges will be harboured, hate nursed.'[18]

A more recent large-scale survey of 'Children's Beliefs about Punishment' in the United States used a representative sample of 200 children with an average age of 10. They were presented with examples of misbehaviour, asked how serious they felt them to be, and told to choose between various forms of punishment. Only a tiny 6.4 per cent of the possible 804 responses advocated physical forms of discipline: 'Interestingly, the most "popular" forms of discipline recommended by these children are exactly those advocated by child development experts: reasoning with children and talking to them about what they did wrong.' Physical punishment was most often advocated as a response to a situation in which a child had 'hit sibling'. The author comments:

> In so far as physical punishment was recommended six times as often in response to aggressive misbehaviour as non-aggressive misbehaviour, it can be concluded tentatively that by middle childhood some children have acquired an association between aggression and physical punishment that is especially strong in the case of family aggression. Thus, these findings lend support for the idea that the family serves as a training ground for violence, with physical punishment playing a prominent role in normalizing aggression against family members for some children.[19]

The deterrent effect of corporal punishment was dismissed by the two official committees in the UK whose reports led to the ending of judicial corporal punishment. The Cadogan Committee in 1938 – after a thorough investigation – concluded that the level of recidivism among birched offenders was at least as high, if not higher than among offenders who had not been birched.[20] And the Barry Committee in 1960 confirmed this, deciding that corporal punishment was not 'an especially effective deterrent to those who have received it or others'.[21] In schools using corporal punishment, the recurrence of the same pupils' names over and over again – often for the same offence – in the books which had to be kept to record punishment was another convincing demonstration of its failure to deter.[22] And also in relation to school corporal punishment, there was research to show that, for example, a high proportion of children beaten for smoking actually increased their cigarette consumption at a time when smoking by children was in decline;[23] and that schools which cane heavily tended to have more delinquency, more classroom mis-behaviour, more vandalism, lower attendance rates and worse examination results than other schools with similar social and intellectual intakes.[24]

## The Links with Child Abuse

People in the UK have never been as concerned as they are now about child abuse. So far, illogically, that concern has not led to action to end or even discourage physical punishment. The links are obvious: all action to cause physical pain to a child, from the little tap to the fatal beating, is on one continuum of violence. The current acceptability of physical punishment causes confusion – where is the line to be drawn? – and makes escalation (given also the ineffective-ness of hitting children) more likely. There is also the demonstrated direct link, namely, that child abusers tend in almost every case to have been severely physically punished themselves.

Where is the clear division between child abuse and 'moderate and reasonable' physical punishment? A recent British handbook *Under-standing Child Abuse*, by the general secretary of the British Association of Social Workers and others, states that it is 'very noticeable that parents who injure their children, at whatever age and however seriously, more often than not relate the event to a concept of punishment, even when they accept that they went "too far" '.[25] American lawyer Dean Herman writes:

If policy-makers and the courts find it difficult to distinguish between 'abuse' and 'appropriate' punishment, we can assume that many parents also find such a distinction difficult to discern. Furthermore, even if parents are aware that they may 'go too far' at times, they often continue to physically punish their children, often out of anger . . . The point is that corporal punishment and child abuse occur along one continuum of violence toward children; the difference between the punishment inflicted by the abuser and by the average American parent is only one of degree, not one of kind.

Once a society declares that the use of violence against children is legitimate, it is difficult to then convince every parent in the society that only an arbitrarily set degree of violence is appropriate and then have them consistently abide by that limit, especially in times of anger or stress. Therefore to work effectively towards the substantial curtailment of child abuse in our society, we must eliminate the foundation of nearly all such abuse: the societal approval of violence inflicted upon children.[26]

Penelope Leach argues in her child-rearing manual *Baby and Child*:

The real danger in physical punishments is that, because they are ineffective in teaching children how they should behave, they tend to escalate. Most of your child's wrongdoing is caused by impulse and forgetfulness. Today you spend all afternoon yelling at him not to run over the flower bed. Finally you smack him. Tomorrow he does the same thing again. Logically you have to smack him again – harder. If you let yourself get into the beginning of that particular vicious circle, this year's smack or half hour in his room can easily become next year's real spanking or hour locked in the toilet.[27]

John and Elizabeth Newson describe the process of escalation in *Four Years Old in an Urban Community:*

The reason for this is easy to understand. Once a mother accepts smacking as a means of discipline suitable for many occasions, and begins to use it often, she thereby debases her own currency of methods of control; that is to say, if smacking is the response to everyday 'naughtiness', she has nothing in reserve for more serious misdemeanours. Because, every now and then, the child will do something which the mother feels needs a special mark of her disapproval, she will therefore tend gradually to increase the severity of her blows, either by hitting harder, or by moving to a more vulnerable part of the body – from legs and bottom to the face, for instance. Most mothers have certain taboos about where they will 'draw the line' in smacking: most suppose that they would never use an implement or slap the child's face, others restrict themselves firmly to the leg or the bottom or the hand; but once the current taboo has been broken, and smacking has escalated to a new level, even for one occasion, that new level has a much better chance than before of becoming the mother's normal practice. This is why frequent smackers are also likely to be objectively hurtful smackers. The process of escalation does not usually continue indefinitely of course; and the reason why much of this evidence comes from *erstwhile* frequent smackers is that there comes a point when the mother is brought up short by a sudden traumatic realization of what she is doing to her relationship with the child.[28]

Two parents interviewed by the Newsons illustrate this:

I'm trying to stop smacking. I did have a time – I don't know how I got into it, every time he used to do something I used to smack him, and it used to be across his cheek; and I know it was wrong. He used to cry after; and for a bit, every time I went to him, he went like this (guarding cheek) – flinch, as though I'd been cruel to him. I knew I didn't ought to, but I did. So I'm trying to stop now, and he's forgotten it, he doesn't do that.

I will admit – I used to smack him and smack him, and I realized it wasn't doing any good. One day, I'd smacked him, and he looked really terrified and he just – 'Oh, not again, Mum – don't!'. He was really terrified of me – I told my husband about it at night – well, he didn't know I did smack him. He doesn't believe in smacking. So I said, 'Well, I don't care how cheeky he gets, I'll never do it again'. And I don't think I have ever smacked him so hard since. I said, 'Well, I was terrified of my mother, and I don't want him to be terrified of me', and I think that did it. He is getting more cheeky, I think, because I've stopped it – I try and talk to him. I don't care how cheeky he gets though: I wouldn't like him to be frightened of me, same as I was of my Mum. But I just remember when I was walking round the yard, and he walked backwards away from me, and he was terrified, and I came in and had a good cry. And I made my mind up; and afterwards worked it out.[29]

When the Committee of Ministers of the Council of Europe adopted a recommendation for action on 'Violence in the Family' in 1985, it proposed that member states (including the UK) should 'review their legislation on the power to punish children in order to limit or indeed prohibit corporal punishment, even if violation of such a prohibition does not necessarily entail a criminal penalty'. The explanatory memorandum to the recommendation described corporal punishment as 'an evil which must at least be discouraged as a first step towards outright prohibition. It is the very assumption that corporal punishment of children is legitimate that opens the way to all kinds of excesses and makes the traces or symptoms of such punishment acceptable to third parties.'[30] This was a reference to the tolerance which doctors and others have shown to significant injuries of children in cultures like our own where physical punishment is still an acceptable practice (see page 33).

In the United States the senior government medical official, the Surgeon General, convened a 'Workshop on Violence and Public Health' in October 1985, and later reported the recommendations to a Senate subcommittee. The working group on 'Child Abuse Prevention' recommended 'a massive campaign to reduce the public acceptance of violence and to protect children against all forms of violence including physical punishment'. A 'No Hitter Day' was one of the techniques proposed, enlisting the help of the media. The working group on 'Assault and Homicide' recommended: 'We should decrease the cultural acceptance of violence by discouraging corporal punishment in the home, forbidding corporal punishment in the school, and abolishing capital punishment by the state because all are models and sanctions of violence.'[31]

The links with child abuse were prominent among the reasons for Sweden's decision to ban physical punishment. In the words of an official of the Ministry of Justice:

. . . there are still great risks that the parent who is used to chastising his child will gradually increase the degree of violence and, one day, will beat the child badly. Most parents who are prosecuted for maltreating their children defend themselves by saying 'I didn't mean to hurt him. I just administered physical punishment which I am entitled to do.' As long as it is not totally clear that a parent may not use physical violence when bringing up a child, it will be difficult to stop or reduce child assault [see page 77].

A graphic, tragic example of the effects of confusion about 'acceptable' levels of violence to children is seen in the inquiry report into the death in 1978 of 8-year-old Lester Chapman.[32] Lester's body was found trapped in sewage sludge about a quarter of a mile from his home. He had died of exposure after running away from home for the fourth time. The search for him had continued for a month and a half, and there was a great deal of national publicity. The report of the independent inquiry into Lester's death revealed that he and other children in the family experienced frequent physical punishment from both his mother and stepfather. He ran away for the first time, the inquiry report stated, after being beaten by his mother with a plastic belt and also probably a plastic toy sword. After he was found, a police constable took him to Reading police station: 'According to the police officer the injuries would have amounted to the offence of causing actual bodily harm, or even that of causing grievous bodily harm, had they not been in the course of chastisement by a mother of her son.' A doctor was called in. He observed 'about eight weals on the right buttock and three on the left, with the skin broken within some of the lesions . . . It was the opinion of the doctor that "the physical injury . . . was of a trivial nature only but perhaps a more severe punishment than one would expect to be given to a child of his age".' A social worker arrived; she spoke to the police and the doctor, and looked at Lester's injuries. All of them reported that they agreed there was no justification for seeking a 'place of safety order' to remove Lester from his home, even temporarily, although Lester made it quite clear that he did not want to go home, and told one policeman that he would run away again. The inquiry report disagrees with the decision, saying there was ample evidence for a place of safety order, although it also says the inquiry team did not feel in a position to question the doctor's clinical judgment.

Lester ran away twice more and was returned home before his final disappearance after school on 12 January 1978. Five children in varying ways described Lester as 'having been very sad on the day before his last schoolday. At lunchtime he told them "I am going to the railway to get killed by a train" . . . Another child remembered him saying that he was "Going to run away and jump in the river", and that he had said he had run away before and nearly fallen in.' Throughout many interviews with social workers, NSPCC inspectors and schoolteachers, his mother and stepfather demonstrated that they regarded physical punishment as normal and essential. His mother indicated that it was a daily occurrence in Lester's short life.

Lester, his parents, and the professionals who failed to act were all affected by the current social norm, namely, the acceptance of hitting children, including hitting them hard and with implements. Lester was the only person to be affected fatally.

The acceptability of physical punishment causes confusion not only to parents and professionals, but also to those who are hit. A study, reported in the international journal *Child Abuse and Neglect* in 1988, shows how a large sample of university students described their experience of physical discipline. Eighty per cent of the students reported being 'spanked', but far fewer reported physical discipline, suggesting that spanking did not even rate as a form of physical punishment for them. And less than 3 per cent described themselves as having been physically abused as a child: astonishingly, only 43 per cent of those who had bones broken in the course of physical discipline classified themselves as physically abused, as did between 35 and 38 per cent of those receiving burns, cuts, dental injuries or head injuries, and 10 per cent of those bruised. (In a very much smaller study, reported in the same paper, of 14-year-old to 17-year-old adolescents who were receiving help from a rural social services department because of documented physical and, in some cases, sexual abuse, only 4 out of 21 described themselves as being physically abused by their parents.)

In their conclusion, the authors describe the rates of severely punitive experiences identified in the research as 'sobering'. But their findings also indicate that personal standards for discipline and abuse vary widely. Follow-up interviews revealed that individuals may describe their own childhood discipline as 'strict' or 'harsh' or 'uncompromising', while they describe the identical discipline of others as 'abusive'. The study suggests 'that even recipients of extremely punitive discipline fail to recognise the inappropriateness of specific acts of discipline'.[33]

This stunning refusal to accept the reality of violent childhood experiences for what they are, makes it all too likely that the recipients will find such methods acceptable and normal when they themselves come to bring up children. It has already been noted just how influential childhood experience of physical punishment is in setting later attitudes to its use (see page 16).

Steele and Pollock, who carried out 'A Psychiatric Study of Parents who Abuse Infants and Small Children', report:

There seems to be an unbroken spectrum of parental action toward children ranging from the breaking of bones and fracturing of skulls through severe bruising to severe spanking and on to mild 'reminder pats' on the bottom . . . we have felt that in dealing with the abused child we are not observing an isolated, unique phenomenon, but only the extreme form of what we would call a pattern or style of child rearing quite prevalent in our culture.[34]

Åke Edfeldt, director of the international study of violence in children's lives carried out during the International Year of the Child, writes in *Violence towards Children* that 'the existing social acceptance of minor physical correctives is the kingsway to a better understanding of the more violent and grave forms of child abuse. I maintain that there is only a difference in degree not in kind between these two groups of phenomena.' Åke Edfeldt sees it as 'a rather treacherous continuum – at one end of the continuum minor physical corrective measures are accepted socially, while an increase in gravity of the same basic behaviour along the continuum results in misdemeanours, becoming eventually felonious at the other end of the continuum. Every attempt to look upon these forms of behaviour as forming two qualitatively separate continua will only add to the difficulties in wiping out the majority of child abuse cases.' If the socially accepted part of the continuum lost its acceptability, 'and was successively replaced by positive reinforcements in the process of upbringing and education, we might assume that the proportion of child abuse cases would greatly decline'. Professor Edfeldt does not, of course, see this as an easy task, but he does believe that in Sweden the 1979 law prohibiting physical punishment has now created sufficient social pressure to make it easier for parents not to use physical punishment than to defend using it.[35]

In *Behind Closed Doors: Violence in the American Family*, authors Richard Gelles, Murray Straus and Suzanne Steinmetz, who have probably been responsible for more research into family violence than anyone else over the last two decades, state their belief in the continuum with physical punishment at one end and child abuse at the other: 'In between are millions of parents whose use of physical force goes beyond mild punishment but which for various reasons does not get identified and labelled as "child abuse".'[36]

A more direct link between physical punishment and child abuse is frequently found when the background to individual reported instances of child abuse, or cases which involve parents being prosecuted, is looked at in detail. In *Spare the Rod*, Jane and James Ritchie suggest that 'there is common agreement that 90 per cent of what are regarded as child abuse cases are committed by parents who simply went too far. Only 10 per cent of child abuse is truly pathological in origin and the rest arises out of the normal context of rather ordinary or common parental practices exacerbated by stressful conditions.' The Ritchies indicate that two research studies of child abuse in New Zealand found that the parents involved were

> . . . generally . . . in unstable, adverse environments and believing that they were justly punishing the child for bad behaviour or misdemeanours . . . When we review the . . . cases in detail, beating is the most frequent form of abuse. In these New Zealand cases the abusive adults beat the children with almost anything that comes to hand: sticks, straps, light cords, cricket bats, chair legs, broom handles, lengths of hose, pieces of wood, hearth brushes, hair brushes, shoes, slippers, belts, buckles, bottles, walking stick, a 'hard object', a 'blunt object' and of course, hands, fist and feet. These attacks are simply an extension of the ordinary violence that starts as a smack on the hand in New Zealand.

They conclude:

> If we used the information we already have which links child abuse to physical punishment we would be well on the road to eliminating both. When that day comes, the Punch and Judy show which is now played out in real life in the kitchens and bedrooms of ordinary homes will cease to have any meaning at all; it will have gone back to where it belongs as a half-forgotten myth about a dangerous possibility we have learnt to avoid.[37]

Another study reported by the Ritchies used a network established by the New Zealand Department of Social Welfare to report on all cases coming to the attention of the authorities. It found, 'as in almost all similar studies, a very high percentage of those who commit child abuse were themselves abused as children'. The first attempt to look intensively at the extent of severe child abuse in a defined population in England – the north-east Wiltshire study in the 1970s – found that 81.8 per cent of men and 68.7 per cent of women who were directly implicated in serious abuse had themselves been subjected to severe or moderate abuse as children. (The study also found that *all* those directly implicated in severe abuse had been subjected to severe or prolonged 'mental abuse' as children.)[38]

More confirmation is found in studies of battered child patients in a Finnish hospital, and of Swedish and Finnish cases of child abuse brought to court in the late 1970s: '. . . in the great majority of cases the perpetrators insisted that they had only used their right to physically punish their child, and they did not consider themselves to have battered their child.'[39]

An intensive review of 66 cases of prosecuted child abuse in the United States, published in 1981, concluded that child abuse most often occurs as 'extensions of disciplinary actions which at some point and often inadvertently crossed the ambiguous line between sanctioned corporal punishment and unsanctioned child abuse'.[40]

In the introduction to the section on 'Violent Parents' in *Violence in the Family*, editors Suzanne Steinmetz and Murray Straus confess to being uncomfortable with the term 'abusive parents', because it tends to focus on what is wrong with the parents as individuals, and to focus attention on the need for treatment to correct the behaviour of particular parents. They refer to an article about an 'abusive', family, the Nolans: 'We do not doubt that parents such as the Nolans need the help of professionals to aid them in ending their mistreatment of a child. But we feel that the roots of this behaviour are to be found in the "normal" social patterns of the society. The Nolans represent an impermissible *extension* of these basic violent tendencies in American society.'[41]

In another paper in the same book, David Gil, described as 'the major figure among researchers and clinicians concerned with child abuse who rejects the psychopathology theory of the causes of child abuse', argues that nationwide studies of child abuse in the United States have revealed that

> . . . physical abuse appears to be endemic in American society since our cultural norms of child rearing do not preclude the use of a certain measure of physical force toward children by adults caring for them . . . Against the background of public sanction of the use of violence against children, it should surprise no one that extreme incidents will occur from time to time in the course of 'normal' child rearing practices. It should be noted that in most incidents of child abuse, the caretakers involved are 'normal' individuals exercising their prerogative of disciplining a child whose behaviour they find is in need of correction. While some of these adults may go further than they intended because

of anger and temporary loss of self-control and/or because of
chance events, their behaviour does, nevertheless, not exceed the
normative range of disciplining children as defined by the
existing culture.

While David Gil sees culturally sanctioned physical force as 'the
basic causal dimension of all violence against children in American
society', he recognises that there are additional dimensions causing
the varying incidence rates of child abuse amongst different social,
economic and ethnic groups. In terms of implications for social
policy

> ... since cultural sanctions of the use of physical force in child
> rearing constitute the common core of all physical abuse of
> children in American society, efforts aimed at gradually changing
> this aspect of the prevailing child rearing philosophy and
> developing clear-cut cultural prohibitions and legal sanctions
> against such use of physical force, are likely to produce over time
> the strongest possible reduction of the incidence and prevalence
> of physical abuse of children.

Like Åke Edfeldt, he realises that this is not going to be easy

> ... for adults who were subjected to physical force and violence
> in their own childhood and who have integrated the existing
> value system of American society. Moreover children can
> sometimes be very irritating and provocative in their behaviour
> and may strain the tolerance of adults to the limit. Yet, in spite of
> these realities, which must be acknowledged and faced openly,
> society needs to work toward the gradual reduction, and
> eventual complete elimination, of the use of physical force
> against children if it intends to protect their basic right of
> security from physical attack.[42]

*Understanding Child Abuse*, referred to earlier (page 21), quotes
David Gil with approval. Covering the possibility of banning
physical punishment in the UK, the authors write:

> Since it seems that most parents at some time beat or threaten
> their children with an implement, it is hardly surprising that any
> suggestion that this is harmful will generate a strong reaction ...
> There is no doubt that our society, more than most other

European societies and other cultures, places a high premium on the infliction of physical pain as necessary or inevitable in the rearing of children. It seems probable that this creates a context in which child abuse is more likely.

The authors go on to advocate wide publicity for 'more humane and effective alternatives' to corporal punishment.[43]

## Dangers of 'Accidental' Injury to Children

It should perhaps be obvious that hitting people – and particularly children – carries the risk of causing physical injury in addition to pain. When a sample of 4,695 American university students were asked about their childhood experience of physical punishment, 12.1 per cent reported that they had been injured in the course of physical discipline by their parents, and 1.9 per cent had received medical services (see page 26).

Penelope Leach, in *Baby and Child*, finds it necessary to warn parents that 'smacks and other physical punishments can be unexpectedly dangerous too. A light smack can catch a child off balance and knock him down; a boxed ear can mean a burst ear drum; while shaking a child while his head is still relatively heavy compared with his body can lead to whiplash injury to his spine and even to concussion.'[44]

An American booklet, *Think Twice: The Medical Effects of Physical Punishment* looks comprehensively at the dangers:

The fine line between discipline and child abuse differs from one family to another and physical punishment is often shockingly at variance with accurate information about the vulnerability of the immature bodies of small children. Spanking is currently accepted by our society as a method of training and socializing children, but frequently children are more seriously injured than intended due to adults' underestimation of the amount of force they can impart. A child may be severely injured by a blow that would only cause minor bruising in an adult. Further, children can be injured unintentionally during even mild punishment if they jerk away and the blows land off target, or if they fall against the sharp edges of furniture or other objects.

The booklet describes injuries to eyes and ears, whiplash injuries to the brain from shaking, to the chest and abdomen, to the buttocks and the genitals.

The booklet also points to the difficulties in researching injuries caused by punishment:

> Only the most serious injuries resulting from punishment come to medical attention, and these are usually said to have resulted from an accident . . . A further difficulty is that many of the consequences of injuries to the brain, internal organs and bones that are received in childhood do not become apparent until months or even years later, long after the punishment is forgotten. Physical and psychological injury are so intricately intertwined during punishment that tracing a developmental impairment to a single cause becomes all but impossible.[45]

The detailed study of severe child abuse in north-east Wiltshire in the 1970s referred to earlier (see page 28) suggested that child maltreatment as a cause of 'impaired intelligence' has not been sufficiently considered. Having looked at all the children under 16 admitted to two mental handicap hospitals in Wiltshire during 1972 and 1973, the authors of the study concluded that 'mentally handicapped children would appear to be more vulnerable to abuse or maltreatment than normal children. Secondly, violence induced (mental) handicap should be recognised as a major cause of mental handicap.'[46]

A startling, if extreme, example of the range of emotional and physical symptoms that can arise in children from physical punishment was revealed in 1983 when a teacher in a small West Virginia town decided to use stern measures to keep her pupils well behaved: children who did not remain in their seats were tied down, those who were not quiet had their mouths taped. The teacher also verbally denigrated pupils and only allowed them to go to the toilets at certain times. Seventeen of the children and their families were then assessed by psychologists. The assessments revealed that over a two-year period of contact with the teacher, the following stress-related symptoms were reported: vomiting, nausea, headaches, stomach-ache, nightmares, ear-ache, fear of the dark, thumb-sucking, crying, bed-wetting and soiling, hair-pulling, insomnia, excessive dependency, difficulty concentrating, excessive shyness, depression, hyper-alertness, fear of strangers, withdrawal, and avoidance of school. One child even pulled out all of her eyelashes. A direct connection was indicated because the symptoms stopped during a three-month period when the teacher was away from school.[47]

Doctors' own attitudes to physical punishment appear to have a significant effect on decisions they may make about reporting or not reporting suspected physical abuse (another dangerous effect of the confusion caused by the acceptance of hitting children discussed earlier – see page 25). Interviews with 58 doctors, reported in the *American Journal of Diseases of Children* in 1985, found their 'tolerance' for physical discipline varied, as did their propensity to report various discipline approaches as abuse: 'Although 98 per cent would recognise bruising with a belt as inappropriate, only half the physicians (48 per cent) said they might report it as abuse. Physicians who indicated a high tolerance for physical discipline . . . also were less likely to report abuse when presented with sample case photographs.' Forty-five per cent of the doctors felt that spanking a child's bottom with an open hand, leaving red marks, was inappropriate as discipline, but only 1 per cent would report it. Eighty-six per cent felt that spanking a bottom leaving bruises was inappropriate, but only 25 per cent would report such an incident. And while 98 per cent felt it was inappropriate to tie up a child as a form of restraint, only 67 per cent would report the practice. The sensitivity of the issue is also emphasised by the fact that only half the doctors asked to participate in a single 20-minute interview for the study agreed to do so.[48] (See also the UK doctor's evaluation of severe injuries caused by physical punishment in the case of Lester Chapman, page 25.)

A senior paediatrician, Dr Edward Christophersen, writing in the journal of the American Academy of Pediatrics in 1980, argued that physicians, educators and child care workers should neither inflict nor sanction corporal punishment: 'However, their responsibility does not end there . . . the pediatrician needs to consider altering his practice to devote more time to counselling parents about normal growth and development, including discipline.'[49]

## Learning to Be Aggressive

Elizabeth and John Newson's interviews with Nottingham mothers of 1-year-olds (see page 54) reflected both the ineffectiveness of physical punishment, and also how aggression was learned:

'I smack her bum. She just turns round and gives you one back' . . . 'Well actually I've smacked her hands – it makes no difference, she just glares at you and does it some more'. . . 'I smack his legs (for many things including screaming, stiffening on the potty,

genital play, throwing things, destructive behaviour). But even
when you smack him sometimes, he doesn't take any notice of
you, he just does it again. And if you smack him he turns round
and smacks you back.'[50]

Norma Feshbach writes in *Child Abuse and Violence*: 'Studies of
child-rearing practices, assessing the effects of parental punishment,
especially the use of physical punishment, yield a consistent outcome.
In general, the degree of parental punitiveness has been found to be
positively correlated with various forms of psychopathology,
especially delinquency and acting-out behaviour.' She accepts the
various reservations that have been raised – the difficulty of
establishing causal links between specific child-rearing practices and
specific behaviour in the child. Do children become delinquent
because they are beaten, or are they beaten because they are
delinquent? 'Nevertheless I am impressed by the degree of consistency
in the findings yielded by very diverse studies of the effects of parental
punishment . . . the predominant finding has been a positive
relationship between physical punishment and aggression.'

Feshbach continues: 'Physical punishment is a source of frustration
and pain, and, as such, it may stimulate anger and aggressive
tendencies. The parent who uses physical aggression in punishing his
child is also serving as an aggressive model. As the work of Bandura
and Walters so clearly reflects, the child, through imitation, may be
acquiring aggressive response patterns although ostensibly being
taught that aggression is bad.[51]

In a submission to the government, arguing against the use of
corporal punishment in schools in the UK, the Association of
Educational Psychologists put it bluntly: 'Children who are beaten
tend in their turn to beat and to bully.'[52] And the British Psychological
Society, in a working group report on corporal punishment in 1980,
said:

There is now a weight of evidence to show that there is a link
between exposure to violence in the real world and acquisition of
violent modes of behaviour . . . Children have a strong tendency,
without which much of their education could scarcely proceed,
to copy the behaviour of their elders . . . A school beating
contains the elements that might be thought to provide a strong
example to the young. A figure in a position of authority solves a
problem of discipline by resorting to physical aggression.[53]

Jane and James Ritchie also summarise the evidence on the side-effects of hitting children in *Spare the Rod*, looking at three areas: the relationship between physical punishment, anger, frustration and aggression; what it is that children learn in punishment situations; and the emotional effects of punishment on children.

There is agreement amongst psychologists engaged in this field that, as the Ritchies explain, 'when a person wants to do something, and is prevented from such action without understanding why, or without any alternative being offered or available, or when they cannot accept the blockage or interference, then anger is the most likely immediate response, even though it may not be outwardly shown'. Thus, when physical punishment is used to stop a child doing something, the first predictable response will be anger:

> Since physical punishment hurts, the anger will be accompanied by pain. So now we not only have an angry child but also one who is hurting. Anger is one side effect; pain is another. A third is apprehension, anxiety or fear. If a child has been hit, he or she may be hit again, so a consequence of the action of hitting is to produce some degree of anxiety. Now we have an angry child who is hurting and also afraid that he or she may be hit again. Three of the most powerful and disturbing human emotions are thus triggered by punishment and the child will be churning with these mixed and confusing emotions.

Until a child learns not to do so

> ... the most likely response to anger and pain is to hit back – this is the natural response of the human organism to such emotions and even when people have learned that they may not or should not act openly, they may still feel like doing so and therefore may seek sneaky or hidden ways of retaliation. Thus physical punishment may lead to children appearing to be suppressed or devious, but most often, the more punished the child, the more aggressive he or she is likely to be.

The Ritchies quote a number of studies reviewing what they term the 'extensive and rather compelling evidence' that children imitate the punisher. Among these they include *Punishment* by G.C. Walters and J.E. Grusec,[54] who say 'if parents employ physical punishment on their children they will become physically aggressive, whereas if they rely on other forms of punishment then children are less likely to become aggressive.'

'There is abundant evidence', write the Ritchies, 'that hitting a child certainly supplies that child with a model for dealing with aggressive behaviour aggressively. He or she will behave in that way with other children.'[55] An example of this is seen in the American research on rates of violence against siblings (see page 59).

An editorial in *Child Abuse and Neglect* in 1982 suggests that there may be a short-term reward in severe physical punishment, but asks what about the long-term effects?

Hurting children to seek a change in behaviour gains rapid results, if the pain is great enough. This is true with adults as well. The main reason this way of changing an adult's behaviour is used seldom in the civilised world is that the negative results are seen so quickly in the form of hitting back, verbal outbursts, law suits, arrest by police etc. The rapid correlation between the initial outburst and the negative response convinces most that this form of modification of one's behaviour is unacceptable.

When children are subjected to pain in order to change their behaviour, on the other hand, the child's behaviour changes long before any negative consequence is realised. The bitterness, loss of self-worth, anger and negative modelling are not seen for years after the insult has occurred. Courts, educators and parents alike find such long-term correlations hard to accept.

Thus the corporal punishment continues because we see only the immediate effect and are blinded to the devastation that this form of discipline produces in our children.[56]

Another American study of a sample of 379 5-year-olds and their mothers, reported in *Violence in the Family*, found, in particular, that physical punishment *for* aggression increased child agression markedly:

Our present data does not tell us why, but we can speculate a little on the reasons. Physical punishment is itself a form of attack – perhaps often perceived as aggression by the child. If parents serve as models, then it is not surprising that the children adopt similar ways of behaving . . . When the parents punish – particularly when they employ physical punishment – they are providing a living example of the use of aggression at the very moment they are trying to teach the child not to be aggressive.

The authors provide clear advice to parents who want to discourage aggressive behaviour: 'A child is more likely to be non-aggressive if his parents hold the value that aggression is undesirable and should not occur. He is more likely to be non-aggressive if his parents prevent or stop the occurrence of aggressive outbursts instead of passively letting them go on, but prevent them by other means than punishment or threats of retaliation.'[57]

Some studies have suggested that it is only high intensities of physical punishment which are linked to aggressive behaviour, and that parents can moderate the effect of physical punishment if they also frequently discuss behaviour with their children. But an American psychologist, who re-analysed interviews with a large representative sample of 1,139 parents with at least one child aged between 3 and 17, concluded in a 1984 paper that, in general, 'moderate physical punishment provides a training ground for violence, a training ground that differs from child abuse only by degree.'[58]

Advice from UK child-rearing advisers also points to the dangers of violence breeding violence. Penelope Leach writes:

A lot of parents believe that a child who deliberately hurts should be hurt back. The idea is that if he is shown what a good smack feels like he will not do it any more. If he does still do it then he deserves painful punishment.

This is a completely illogical argument from the child's point of view. If he smacks you and you smack him back, he sees you have done exactly the same thing as him. He cannot possibly take you seriously when you punctuate your slaps with 'I will *not* have you *hitting* people!'[59]

And Miriam Stoppard advises parents whose child starts to show signs of aggression: 'Don't punish and don't smack your child; this will only make the aggressive behaviour worse.'[60]

One particularly compelling study of the cycle of violence from generation to generation in the United States, the 'Rip Van Winkle Study', began in 1960 when all the third-grade school children (roughly 870 8-year-olds) in a semi-rural county in New York State were assessed, and about 80 per cent of their parents interviewed. Ten years later about half of the original group (now aged 19) were interviewed again. Then, in 1981, 295 of the original group – now aged 30 – were interviewed individually, and another 114 by post. The authors of the study report that

Our data, collected over three generations, indicate that aggression, as characteristic behaviour, is transmitted from parent to child. In the original study, there was a significant relation between how aggressive the children were rated by their peers in schools, and how severely they were punished for aggression by their parents at home. When the group were 19, they were asked how they would respond to aggression if they had an eight-year-old child, and in 1981, those subjects who actually had children aged between six and 12 were asked the same question: there were highly significant correlations between their own peer-nominated aggression and their attitude to their own hypothetical or real children, and also between their parents' response to aggression and their own response 20 years later.[61]

Leonard Eron reports the findings of a three-year longitudinal study of about 600 children in Chicago, which was replicated in Finland, Poland, Holland, Australia and Israel. His paper, in the *American Psychologist* in 1982, states that in the United States, Finland and Poland (the only three countries in the study which had been analysed by then), 'physical punishment by parents relates significantly to aggression of both boys and girls'.[62]

An intriguing study of playground behaviour of children and parents in Germany, Italy and Denmark (organised by two psychologists at the Albert Einstein College of Medicine in New York, Leopold Bellak and Maxine Antell) was provoked by a study of books on the Nazi period in Germany, including biographies showing that nearly all the Nazi criminals had suffered some sort of serious mistreatment or cruelty in childhood. Perhaps, as Leopold Bellak says in a previous book, 'man's inhumanity to man is his revenge for the indignities he suffered in his childhood'. The authors suggest that the study showed a clear association between parent aggression and child aggression, 'that people avenge the abusive and humiliating treatment they receive from their own parents by humiliating others . . . that children learn aggressive behaviour by modelling themselves on aggressive parents'. Pairs of psychologists (working independently and unaware of the hypothesis which they were helping to test) observed groups of children and adults in playgrounds in three cities of roughly comparable size and character – Frankfurt, Copenhagen and Florence. The authors of the study acknowledge that there were all sorts of problems about the method, the samples, the interpretation, and so on. The results, however, are striking and at least suggestive: 'The dramatically greater aggressiveness of the treatment of German children shown in this experiment fits the notion widely held by Germans themselves that German culture is *kinderfeindlich*, or hostile to children.' The Danish and Italian children and their parents, on the other hand, showed consistently low aggression scores.

This is an extract from the verbatim notes recorded by one of the observers in a Frankfurt playground:

12.15:  f pushing e;

e yelling, shouting to f;

k on the top of the grating, laughing at d, singing: 'Silly little Petrus!', repeated several times;

d coming up to the grating, interested in climbing;

e and f and k stop playing, jump down;

d tries to climb;

e flogs d brutally, laughing;

d tries to escape, confused:

12.17:  e looking whether d's trousers are wet, laughing, shouting at d;

e pushes d into the sandbox, throws sand in d's face;

d, weeping softly, throws a little bit of sand back to e;

e and f and k laughing at d;

k kicking on the ground and with her feet pushing sand at d;

f doing the same as k;

d doesn't defend himself anymore, standing immobile weeping;

e and f and k take an elastic and a ball. They have a discussion, can't agree on any game;

d running away;

k pursues d, catches him, flogs d brutally, pulls his arm, pulls him back to e and f,

d resigned, weeping softly;

e and f and k notice the observers, ask what they are doing, a confused situation follows . . .

The authors note that there are other indications of a greater need for aggressive outlet in Germany: the rate of road accidents and all other accidents, of suicide and self-inflicted injuries, and of murder are all much higher in Frankfurt than in Florence or Copenhagen.[63]

## Extreme Pathological Behaviour and Physical Punishment

Alice Miller's passionate book, *For Your Own Good: The Roots of Violence in Child-Rearing*, proposes that 'every act of cruelty, no matter how brutal and shocking, has traceable antecedents in its perpetrator's past'.[64] She uses the childhoods of three people to explain and justify her theory – those of Adolf Hitler ('representative of extreme destructiveness on a world-historical scale'), Christiane F., the teenage drug addict ('representative of extreme self-destructiveness on a personal scale'), and Jurgen Bartsch, tried in Germany in the late 1960s for a series of 'indescribably cruel' child murders. All three 'were subjected to severe humiliation and mistreatment as children'.

Alice Miller indicates that in her studies of all the leading figures of the Third Reich, she has not been able to find a single one who did not have a strict and rigid upbringing. 'Shouldn't that give us a great deal of food for thought?' She believes that the example of Hitler's childhood allows us to study 'the genesis of a hatred whose consequences caused the suffering of millions'; biographers have tried to exonerate Hitler's parents – Miller sees his childhood as 'anticipating the concentration camps': 'Little Adolf could be certain of receiving constant beatings; he knew that nothing he did would have any effect on the daily thrashings he was given. All he could do was deny the pain, in other words deny himself and identify with the aggressor. No one could help him, not even his mother, for this would spell danger for her too, because she was also battered.' Hitler was not an isolated phenomenon: 'He would not have had millions of followers if they had not experienced the same sort of upbringing.' Alice Miller was expecting great resistance to her thesis when *For Your Own Good* was first published in Germany in 1980, 'so I was surprised to discover how many readers, both young and old, agreed with me. They were familiar from their own backgrounds with what I depicted. I didn't have to adduce elaborate arguments; all I needed to do was describe Hitler's childhood in such a way that it served as a mirror, and suddenly Germans caught their own reflections in it.'

She did, of course, receive reactions reflecting the attitude 'it didn't do *me* any harm': ' "Basically, my childhood differed little from Hitler's; I too had a very strict upbringing, was beaten and mistreated. Why then didn't I become a mass murderer instead of, say, a scientist, a lawyer, a politician or a writer?" ' Alice Miller argues that her book provides clear answers:

e.g. Hitler never had a single other human being in whom he could confide his true feelings; he was not only mistreated but also prevented from experiencing and expressing his pain; he didn't have any children who could have served as objects for abreacting his hatred; and, finally, his lack of education did not allow him to ward off his hatred by intellectualizing it. Had a single one of these factors been different, perhaps he would never have become the arch-criminal he did.

Christiane F. lived her first six years in the country on a farm; then her family moved to Berlin, to a small apartment on the 12th floor of a high-rise block: 'The sudden loss of a rural setting, of familiar playmates, and of all the free space that goes with living in the country is in itself hard enough for a child, but it is all the more tragic if the child must come to terms with this loss all by herself, and if she is constantly faced with unpredictable punishment and beatings.' From her own account of her childhood, Christiane was often beaten for reasons she does not understand:

> . . . finally [she] begins to act in ways that give her father 'good reason to beat her'. By so doing, she improves his character by making an unjust and unpredictable father into one who at least punishes justly. This is the only way she has to rescue the image of a father she loves and idealizes. She also begins to provoke other men and turn them into punitive fathers – first the building superintendent, then her teachers, and finally, during her drug addiction, the police . . . As time goes by, Christiane does to herself what her father had done to her earlier; she systematically destroys her self-respect, manipulates her feelings with the use of drugs, condemns herself to speechlessness (this highly articulate child) and isolation and in the end ruins body as well as soul.

Jurgen Bartsch was removed from his tubercular mother immediately after delivery in 1946; he stayed in hospital for 11 months. His adoptive mother beat him; acquaintances of the family noticed that he was always black and blue. He was also locked up in a cellar with barred windows and artificial light for long periods; later, he lured small boys into an underground shelter and killed them in unspeakable ways.

In passing, Alice Miller refers to Mary Bell, convicted in England in 1968 at the age of 11 of murdering two other children. Miller alleges that her mother rejected her after birth; that the mother 'made whipping people her profession', and 'tormented, threatened and probably tried to kill her own child'. (Gitta Sereny's book, *The Case of Mary Bell*, suggests that Mary Bell's mother tried to kill her daughter four times.)[65]

Alice Miller uses the term 'poisonous pedagogy' to describe the violent child-rearing which she sees as the root of cruelty and violence in society:

> We will continue to infect the next generation with the virus of 'poisonous pedagogy' as long as we claim that this kind of upbringing is harmless . . . we can protect ourselves from a poison only if it is clearly labelled as such, not if it is mixed, as it were, with ice cream advertised as being 'For Your Own Good' . . . When people who have been beaten or spanked as children attempt to play down the consequences by setting themselves up as examples, even claiming it was good for them, they are inevitably contributing to the continuance of cruelty in the world by this refusal to take their childhood tragedies seriously. Taking over this attitude, their children, pupils and students will in turn beat their own children, citing their parents, teachers and professors as authorities.

Alice Miller insists that in all she has read about the childhood of criminals, of mass murderers, 'I have been unable to find anywhere the beast, the evil child whom pedagogues believe they must educate to be "good". Everywhere I find defenceless children who were mistreated in the name of child-rearing, and often for the sake of the highest ideals.'

She believes that behind every crime 'a personal tragedy lies hidden'.

> We are still barely conscious of how harmful it is to treat children in a degrading manner. Treating them with respect and recognising the consequences of their being humiliated are by no means intellectual matters, otherwise, their importance would long since have been generally recognised . . . We don't yet know, above all, what the world might be like if children were to grow up without being subjected to humiliation, if parents would respect them and take them seriously as persons. In any case, I don't know of a single person who enjoyed this respect as a child and then as an adult had the need to put other human beings to death.

The authors of *Behind Closed Doors* summarise studies linking violence in childhood with later extreme aggression:

> Researchers who have studied child abuse continue to find that children who were abused often grow up to be abusing parents . . . Research on murderers finds that killers experienced more frequent and severe violence as children than their brothers who did not go on to commit a homicide. Examinations of presidential assassins or would-be assassins also find these individuals sharing common histories of violent upbringing. In his diary, Arthur Bremer, Governor George Wallace's would-be assassin wrote, "My mother must have thought I was a canoe, she paddled me so much." Lee Harvey Oswald, Sirhan Sirhan and Charles Manson all experienced violent childhoods. A study of violent inmates of San Quentin prison found that 100 per cent of them experienced extreme violence between the ages of one and 10 . . .[66]

## Clear Association with Delinquency

John and Elizabeth Newson have analysed their Nottingham research on child-rearing to see if there are links between children's experiences of punishment in early life and the way they actually turn out. They found a 'very clear association' between the frequency of physical punishment at 11 and the child's perceived delinquency. As they comment: 'This poses a question: are these children delinquent because they are smacked, or are they smacked because they are delinquent? The question cannot be answered; what we *can* say however is that smacking and beating mothers do not succeed in producing non-delinquent children, and the dictum of "spare the rod and spoil the child" can't be upheld by these findings.' The Newsons also found that: 'Parents who use physical punishment as a deliberate disciplinary strategy are not significantly more likely than the parents who feel "driven" to smack to have children who kick over the traces. It also appears, however, that they are not actually more successful in producing "good" children than parents who manage to avoid habitual resort to physical punishment.'

Looking at 'troublesomeness' at 16, in relation to parental punishment at 7, the Newsons found: ' "Spare the rod and spoil the child" carries still less weight: troublesomeness at 16 is clearly not prevented by the mother having smacked, beaten or generally relied on punishment at seven; in fact children are more likely to be troublesome at 16 if they were smacked frequently or beaten at seven.' The Newsons emphasise that the links persist when the effects of class and sex are set aside. And, finally, they have looked at possible associations between various child-rearing variables at the age of 7 and 11 and an eventual criminal record:

> Those which are of particular importance are those which still 'shine through' as having significance even when we set aside the effects of class, sex and family size; those which do shine through can be fairly assumed to be causative in their association. The measures which stand out as being most predictive of criminal record before the age of 20 are having been smacked or beaten once a week or more at 11, and having had a mother with a high degree of commitment to formal corporal punishment at that age.

They also indicate that 'father's – non-punishing – involvement with the child at 11 stands out as *protecting* the child from acquiring a criminal record in adolescence'.[67]

One American psychologist, Ralph Welsh, who has become convinced of the links between physical punishment and delinquency over a long period, has gone so far as to offer a $100 reward to any probation or court officer who can bring him a male recidivist delinquent who has not received severe parental punishment. In correspondence in 1983 with a clinical psychologist in England, Dr Ludwig Lowenstein, who had written an article advocating the use of physical punishment in certain circumstances, Dr Welsh writes: 'As you know, I have seen more than two thousand juvenile delinquents in my career. I still see an average of four delinquents a week, and I find it remarkable that I have yet to find the first recidivist male delinquent that wasn't raised on a belt, board, cord or fist; such individuals simply do not exist.'[68]

Ralph Welsh has developed what he has termed 'The belt theory of juvenile delinquency' (most recently expounded – together with a summary of other research linking parental physical punishment to solvent and alcohol abuse, sexual abuse and maladjustment, and depression – at the 96th annual convention of the American Psychological Association, Atlanta, Georgia in August 1988):

1  The level of reported aggressive behaviour in males is a function of the severity of their corporal punishment histories.

2 Severity of corporal punishment in the home is more important than socio-economic class as a precursor to delinquency.

3 Corporal punishment produces both fear and anger; when the fear habituates, anger is left in its place.

4 The more aggressive a culture, the more probable the members of that culture will be found to utilise corporal punishment as their chief socialisation technique.

5 Since the effects of corporal punishment are no respecter of group, race or social class, so-called normal parents will have aggressive children proportional to the severity of corporal punishment they utilize on their offspring.

6 Parents of delinquents are, contrary to popular opinion, 'hard-liners' on discipline rather than over-permissive, although they are often neglectful; permissiveness and neglect are not the same.

7 Although severe parental punishment appears to be a necessary precursor to delinquent aggression, family violence, especially between the parents, produces a powerful modelling effect, accentuating the anger already implanted in the child.

8 The well-documented differences in conditionability between delinquents and 'normals' are probably due to fear habituation, reducing the delinquent's ability to rely on anticipatory fear responses, and avoid potentially delinquent situations. It is speculated that this process of habituation or 'negative perception' is primarily due to the delinquent's early exposure to severe parenting.

9 Poverty appears to be a major source of frustration in families with high rates of delinquency. However, poverty probably produces crime indirectly, apparently acting as a catalyst for aggressive parenting.

Ralph Welsh says that he has 'repeatedly suggested that all belt manufacturers stamp on the back of their belts: "Caution: the use of this belt on your child is dangerous to his mental health." ' He also asks each delinquent referred to his office what the world would be like if all parents stopped spanking their children: '100 per cent of my sample reports that it would be utter chaos, with people killing, stealing and robbing from each other . . . Clearly delinquents believe in corporal punishment, are convinced that their parents hit them because they were bad, and believe they are as bad as they are because their parents let some things slide and didn't hit them enough.' Thus hitting children emphasises the acceptability of hitting. This finding is also confirmed by the American research which showed that children, whose parents had broken bones in the course of punishing them, still denied that they had been abused (see page 26).[69]

In a progress report on a study of the *Relationship of Family Patterns to Child Behaviour Disorders*, carried out for the US Public Health Service in 1960, Albert Bandura indicated that most criminally aggressive youngsters come from families where the parents may have no criminal background, but used physical punishment within the 'normal range'.[70] Another study looked at the background of 97 imprisoned juvenile delinquents in the United States in 1979; 78 of them had been responsible for serious violence. It found that 75 per cent of the violent delinquents had been physically abused as children; 33 per cent of the non-violent delinquents had also experienced physical abuse.[71]

In Sweden, Tor Sverne, the judge who chaired the Children's Rights Commission when it proposed a ban on all physical punishment (see page 71), indicates that his long experience in the courts revealed that 'few children have had as much chastisement at home as those who are convicted of criminal offences'.

## Other Side-effects

It is not just aggression and delinquency that have been found to be linked with physical punishment. Studies – summarised by Dean Herman and others – have also linked it with stealing, truancy, temper, hostile disobedience, development of an authoritarian personality, lying, destructiveness, wife-beating, depression, alcohol and solvent abuse, and racism.[72]

A common factor is the poor development of internal standards and controls in children who are punished physically. Dean Herman writes:

> Those parents who rely on the use or the threat of the use of physical punishment tend to have children whose behaviour is governed not by internal standards but by fear, and these parents will therefore be compelled to retain this fear ... children who fear physical punishment for their transgressions tend to have less guilt over their improper behaviour, less willingness to confess and accept blame for such behaviour, less resistance to temptation and, in general, a lower internal orientation than

children whose parents tend not to rely on physical punishment.

Those taught to limit their behaviour through fear tend to have poor control over their actions when a sufficient degree of fear is no longer present. Such results not only point to the ineffectiveness of physical punishment, as already discussed (page 16), but also leave the growing children who have suffered it prone to all sorts of undesirable adult problems.[73]

Murray Straus, in a survey of American undergraduates, found that students whose parents most emphasised self-control in their children had experienced the least corporal punishment. Students whose parents emphasised that they should think for themselves experienced the second lowest frequency of corporal punishment.[74]

A 1974 study, which looked at parents' occupation and attitudes in relation to their use of physical punishment, revealed that students who ranked 'obedience' as the trait which their parents considered to be the most important had higher physical punishment scores than others. Where parents valued obedience in their child, and were also working in occupations where their belief in obedience was reinforced by a rigid hierarchy and obedience from those 'below' them, even higher rates of physical punishment were found. The study also found, using standard psychological tests, that the children of these parents tended to have 'closed minds'.[75]

In contrast, Norma Feshbach draws attention to the promising results of reinforcing positive and non-aggressive behaviour in children, as exemplified, for example, in the work of two American psychologists[76] who were attempting to modify aggressive behaviour in nursery school settings: 'Nursery school teachers were instructed to ignore aggressive acts whenever possible and to direct their attention to non-aggressive, co-operative behaviours. Changes in the behaviour of the groups reflected a significant and substantial decline in the frequency with which children engaged in physical and in verbal aggression.'[77]

An article in a recent issue of the *Journal of Child Psychology and Psychiatry* begins: 'Harsh discipline of children has been shown to be associated with an increased rate of children's behaviour problems and delinquency, and to forecast adult psychiatric disorder and crime.' It goes on to describe a study showing that 'unfair, harsh and inconsistent discipline by parents predicted alcohol and depressive disorders independently of the effects of parental psychiatric history, and of the respondent's sex and the severity of childhood behaviour problems'. It concludes:

Many of the parental practices found to be deleterious would not qualify as gross neglect or abuse. Nonetheless, they . . . appeared to have had long-term adverse effects. These observations suggest that improvement in ordinary day-to-day handling of children's misbehaviour by parents might have a very broadly beneficial outcome for mental health, and efforts in this direction should not be restricted to the severe cases that now allow prosecution of parents and removal of their children from the home.[78]

Just as physical punishment may cause extreme aggression and sadism, it may also cause masochism. The child who is spanked may find such treatment sexually gratifying both in childhood and later as an adult. The Society of Teachers Opposed to Physical Punishment (STOPP) – the organisation which campaigned for an end to school beating, see Chapter 5 – periodically received letters from individuals who as children had been beaten at home or at school or, in some cases, both, and as adults found their sexual lives obsessed with sado-masochistic fantasies. STOPP drew attention to the large variety of readily available pornography featuring details of home and school beating, and the experience of prostitutes providing 'specialist services' of strict discipline. The extent of the market for such material and services indicates how many people in the UK derive sexual pleasure from sado-masochistic fantasies. One of the cane manufacturers who supplied both schools and parents also published a monthly magazine, *Family View*, which usually contained long descriptions of physical punishment by correspondents describing themselves as parents (see page 120).

Ian Gibson – whose book, *The English Vice: Beating, Sex and Shame in Victorian England and After*, looks in detail at the sexual dangers of physical punishment – finds that the adherence of the British 'to the belief that children are spoiled when the rod, or the threat of the rod, is spared' is 'extraordinary'. Having reviewed the evidence, he concludes: 'It is now 350 years since the publication of Meibom's treatise on the sexual element in flagellation, and nearly 100 years since the appearance of Krafft-Ebing's *Psychopathia Sexualis*. We *know* that beating is sexually dangerous.'[79] Krafft-Ebing wrote in 1886: 'On account of the dangers to which this form of punishment gives rise, it would be better if parents, teachers and nurses were to avoid it entirely.'[80] Freud, Havelock Ellis and many others have confirmed this from the experiences of their patients.

Inevitably, the legalised physical punishment of children by parents and other carers provides a relatively easy outlet for a minority of sadistic adults, just as legalised school beating did until very recently. But the practice also feeds a large-scale and very sordid pornographic industry.

# CHAPTER 2

---

# HOW OFTEN ARE CHILDREN HIT?

*'The majority of British parents we have interviewed seem to believe that physical punishment is an inevitable and probably necessary aspect of ordinary child upbringing.'*

(John and Elizabeth Newson, in Neil Frude (ed.),
*Psychological Approaches to Child Abuse*, 1980)

In the UK and in many parts of the world where our colonial influence has been strongest – for example, the United States, Canada, Australia, New Zealand and South Africa – hitting children as a form of punishment remains socially acceptable. Whenever the practice is investigated in these countries, it is found that most parents still hit their children at least occasionally, and that many parents hit their children frequently, often with implements such as canes, belts, slippers, etc.

Most of this research inevitably relies on interviews with parents, which must surely mean that the statistics produced are under- rather than over-estimates. In a few studies, older children themselves have been asked about their experiences of physical punishment (see page 20). In Finland, results should shortly be available of a large-scale and detailed survey of Finnish schoolchildren's self-reported experiences of physical punishment, and sexual harassment and abuse (see page 90).

But despite the social acceptability of hitting children, there has been some considerable resistance to research into the prevalence of the habit. For example, when in 1979 – the International Year of the Child – Swedish professor Åke Edfeldt was asked to lead an international study of violence towards children, he found the subject was 'taboo' for many people: 'Thus it was difficult to find interview subjects willing to communicate even a part of their thinking on the subject.' The study hoped to involve 40 countries:

What we did not take into consideration was that this whole problem area is so tinged with guilt that both authorities and individual experts alike prefer to leave it alone. There seems to be no better explanation of the fact that the most frequent reply by far to our repeated letters of invitation to participate in the study has been total silence. Some experts and authorities have in general words protested that the chosen . . . technique is inadequate, while others have promised to contribute, but have then failed to do so. In some of these no-show cases it was said that nobody dared to engage in the data-collecting for fear of professional or political reprisals. Only a few organisations, as eg the National Union of Teachers in Britain, openly declared war against the project and forbade their members to have any part in it. The fact that we have British material at all is due to a more than usually unyielding interviewer who managed in the end to get together a complete official British contribution.[1]

As late as 1979, the NUT was still strongly defending the right of British teachers to use corporal punishment in schools.

Most people's experience of how 'the average child' is treated and punished comes from those depressing incidents in bus queues, supermarkets and other public places. The frequency of the incidents, and the general lack of any intervention, illustrates the social acceptability of the practice. In Scandinavian countries where there is a clear ban on physical punishment, accompanied in most cases with a lot of public education, you simply never see children being hit or shaken, and you never hear words like 'Just wait till we get home . . .' (see Chapter 3, page 67).

An impressionistic survey of parental behaviour was reported by a clinical child psychologist, Valerie Yule, in an article in *New Society* in 1985:

I carried out my own study in the streets, shops and buses of a provincial city. I watched a series of adult–child pairs for three minutes each, all of them matched with another pair of people for comparison. There were 85 of each set of pairs. I watched them on sunny afternoons, in places that were not crowded and not at peak hours, so that people were not busy hurrying, or dodging in the traffic. The pairs that did not include a small child might be male/female, all-female or all-male. They ranged from teenage to elderly. But whoever they were, within my three-minute observation period, four-fifths had some speech together, or at least a glance or a smile. All their behaviour towards each other was courteous . . . By contrast, only a quarter of the child–adult pairs had any communication within two minutes of watching, and under half within three minutes. For two-fifths of my sample, what took place was negative. This is what happened:

Seven adults crossed roads telling their children to look out or hurry up, but none of them looked at the child they were speaking to. Five yanked the child by arm or hand.

Six children cried in pushers. Three were smacked, two given sweets round the side of the pusher without a glance at them, and one was ignored.

Four children in shops were told to behave themselves in varying degrees of severity, and one was then pacified with sweets.

Four children on buses were scolded or smacked for misbehaviour, following complete inattention.

Four children at bus stops were told to behave or keep still, and one was cuffed.

Four children tried to talk to adults who paid no attention.

Three children tried to talk to adults and were rejected.

Three children had their clothes adjusted on buses without one word spoken.

Two children were pulled out of pushers without any prior warning.

Two men talked to their small children as they walked along the street.

One child in a bus cried and was ignored.

One mother talked to her child about going home, without looking at it.

One grandmother talked to a seven-year-old about buying mother a birthday present.

One mother in a bus pointed out to a three-year-old child all the sights through the window, with a lively discussion together.

One (Asian) mother in the bus watched her baby's face as she cuddled it.

Eight adult couples chatted while one pushed a pusher containing a wakeful but passive toddler.

For the rest, the adults took no notice of the children they were with, even in some pairs that I watched for up to 10 minutes.

Valerie Yule suggests that this picture of widespread adult rudeness to children is unlikely to be local: 'It fits in with too many current stereotypes in the media for one to dismiss it too easily.' Recalling a series of cartoons in the *Guardian* by Heath, showing parents perceiving their child as a gigantic monster, 'I privately draw my parallel cartoon of the real situation. The child, accurately, sees the parents as gigantic and untrustable owners, who behave in a distracted and unnecessary fashion.'[2]

## Physical Punishment Rates in the UK

The most comprehensive, and apparently the only significant, available information on how often parents hit their children in the UK comes from John and Elizabeth Newson's long-term study of child-rearing practices in a random sample of 700 indigenous Nottingham families. (Families of Afro-Caribbean and Asian origin were excluded from the sample 'in the interests of homogeneity'.) The Newsons are directors of the Child Development Research Unit at the University of Nottingham, and their work has involved interviewing mothers in considerable depth on many aspects of child-rearing including discipline, in their own homes as the children reached their first, fourth, seventh, eleventh and sixteenth birthdays (the samples were made up to 700 at each age-state). Two hundred of the families were followed up when the children were 19. The project began in 1958/59, so the children are now in their thirties and producing a second generation; the interviews continue.

The interviewing methods have been carefully refined to enable mothers to be frank and detailed in their replies, and as the Newsons comment

> ... where we are discussing punishment in general and smacking or beating in particular, the interview method has special strength, in that mothers are extremely unlikely to say that they hit the child if they do not. This means that if our findings are not an accurate record of what mothers actually do, they are inaccurate in a conservative direction; we may have underestimated the extent of physical punishment, but not overestimated.[3]

John and Elizabeth Newson's conclusion is: 'The majority of British parents we have interviewed seem to believe that physical punishment is an inevitable and probably necessary aspect of ordinary child upbringing.'[4] Their findings for the various age-groups studied in the project are summarised below.

They first wrote about their sample of 700 families in *Infant Care in an Urban Community*.[5] The interviews with mothers of 1-year-old children revealed that 62 per cent smacked their babies; 38 per cent never smacked (and indeed many of these were outraged at the suggestion that they might); and 7 per cent reported that they only smacked when the child was in danger. Although this particular study was carried out over 20 years ago, the Newsons emphasise that 'from our current investigations we have no reason to suppose that the extent of physical punishment has decreased across the board'. In a new study, completed in 1985, they interviewed a contemporary random sample of 344 mothers of 1-year-old babies. Preliminary analysis reveals that 63 per cent reported smacking their 1-year-olds, thus confirming the Newsons' belief that the norm has not changed, despite greatly increased publicity and discussion about the dangers of physical abuse.[6]

By the time the children in the original sample of 700 had reached the age of 4, only 3 per cent of the mothers never smacked; and only a quarter smacked less than once a week. A massive majority of children of this age were smacked between once and six times a week, and 7 per cent were smacked once a day or more. The overwhelming majority of mothers of 4-year-olds stated that they believed in smacking – 83 per cent against 17 per cent who disapproved in principle. In their book, *Four Years Old in an Urban Community*, the Newsons discuss the evidence which they collected on the smacking of 4-year-olds:

> The first general finding is that smacking is in general used in dealing with four-year-olds to a very considerable extent; three-quarters of all mothers smacking on average at least once a week, many of them a good deal more often, adds up to a very large number of aggressive acts, whether or not the smacks themselves are objectively painful. We have . . . no way of judging this last dimension; however, on the basis of the verbatim transcripts, we would tentatively suggest that those mothers who smack most frequently are also likely to smack hardest. Not only do the frequent smackers talk as if their smacks hurt more . . . but further evidence from some mothers who *used* to smack often, and no longer do so, supports this hypothesis.[7]

The Newsons see 7 as a key age for looking at smacking attitudes:

Mothers of four-year-olds often say that they have to smack because the child does not understand them well enough for words to have much effect. At seven, this is no longer true, and one would expect smacking to decrease, as it does: the 75 per cent who smacked at least once a week at four are reduced to 41 per cent at seven. However, just because these mothers are now a minority, and because smacking is no longer considered so necessary, the 41 per cent must be considered to be more strongly committed to smacking as a method than were the 75 per cent who smacked as often at four.

At the age of 7, they found that 11 per cent of the boys and 6 per cent of the girls (8 per cent overall) were being smacked once a day or more; a further 33 per cent were being smacked once a week or more, but less than once a day, and only 31 per cent were being smacked less than once a month.

Also by the age of 7, 26 per cent of the boys and 18 per cent of the girls (22 per cent overall) had been hit with an implement. A further 53 per cent (65 per cent of boys and 41 per cent of girls) had been threatened with an implement. (The Newsons found that the implements used or threatened in order of preference were: first, strap or belt; second, cane or stick; third, slipper; fourth, miscellaneous objects – rulers, backs of hairbrushes, etc.)

Thus overall – perhaps the most chilling statistic of all – 91 per cent of the boys and 59 per cent of the girls, or three-quarters of the whole sample, had been hit or threatened with an implement by the age of 7.

By the age of 11, smacking had decreased considerably, with only 3 per cent being hit once or more a day, and 18 per cent at least once a week. Sixty per cent were now being smacked less than once a month or never. However, an implement was being used to beat 15 per cent of the boys and 3 per cent of the girls (9 per cent overall), and a further 5 per cent were 'seriously threatened' with an implement.

## Analysing Prevalence by Class and Other Factors

The Newsons looked at the use of physical punishment, and attitudes to its use, in relation to social class. Given existing stereotypes about child-rearing, it will surprise some people that they found limited significance in class differences. (Research in the United States and New Zealand has confirmed that there is no simple connection between social class and proneness to use physical punishment – see below.) Those classified as 'professional and managerial' (classes I and II) were more likely not to hit their 1-year-old child (56 per cent compared with 38 per cent overall). By the age of 4, hardly any parents were not smacking at all, but class I and II mothers were more likely to smack 'rarely'. But a majority of 4-year-olds in all social classes are smacked at least once a week, up to six days a week. There are no significant class differences in the proportion of mothers who believe in smacking 4-year-olds, which averages out at an overwhelming majority of 83 per cent. With 7-year-olds, sex differences of the children are more significant than class differences in relation to the frequency of smacking.

Looking at the use or threat of an implement on 7-year-olds, class differences are insignificant, but it is in classes I and II that the proportion of mothers who admit to having used an implement is highest (25 per cent as against 18 per cent in class IV and 17 per cent in class V). The difference in the experience of boys and girls is dramatic, especially in white-collar families. These particularly favour the use of implements on their boys ('a swingeing 97 per cent'), but use them much less on their girls (55 per cent).

Mothers' reliance on physical punishment was measured at the time their children were 7 and 11 by studying the answers to a series of questions. Reliance on hitting does increase across the social-class scale from class I to class V, but again differences according to the child's sex are far more significant, with 40 per cent of 7-year-old boys overall having mothers who rely heavily on corporal punishment, compared with 23 per cent of girls. By the age of 11, only 17 per cent of classes I and II are highly committed to formal corporal punishment. The other classes are more closely bunched, but the white-collar group (class III, white collar) is the only one showing a majority who are highly committed to the formal corporal punishment of boys (54 per cent, as against 23 per cent committed to it for girls). When the social class analysis is summarised as middle class versus working class, there is no significant difference in their commitment to formal corporal punishment.

The Newsons also report two smaller parallel studies, involving interviews with 200 families of Punjabi origin and 200 families of Afro-Caribbean origin, and plotting the frequency of physical punishment with 7-year-old children. These showed that the parents of Punjabi origin resorted hardly at all to hitting, whereas parents of Afro-Caribbean origin 'punish their children still more frequently and severely than do indigenous white parents'. The Newsons note:

It is perhaps salutary to remind ourselves that historically West Indian parents derive their values from a hierarchical and rigid social system which institutionalized and condoned slave labour and the physical beating of slaves by our own forebears. Additionally, West Indian culture has since been influenced by a strong commitment to a revivalist religion (also imported from Britain) which stresses that pain to the body is of far less concern than damnation of the soul.

And their general conclusion is that 'parents in Britain who habitually resort to physical punishment can be seen to be conforming to a cultural norm'.[8]

In the 1980s Urie Bronfenbrenner wrote an influential article in the United States which concluded that frequent use of physical punishment was more characteristic of working-class families, and that the middle classes tended to use reasoning, isolation and love-oriented techniques.[9] This (comfortable for the middle classes) assumption seems to have prevailed for a few years until Howard Erlanger challenged the empirical basis for Bronfenbrenner's view and took a careful look at other studies. His conclusion was that the relationship between social class and the use of spanking is relatively weak – 'not strong enough to be of great theoretical or practical significance'. He points out that a survey done for a US Commission into Violence found that 'contrary to popular belief poorly educated whites are the only group of parents with a high rate of outright rejection of spanking'. The implication of Erlanger's work is to challenge any suggestion that 'lower class persons "typically" use physical punishment to control children, whereas middle class persons "typically" use other means'. He refers to the obvious factors which may lead to families without resources – suffering from unemployment, poverty, poor housing, etc. – using physical punishment, although they may be no more pre-disposed to its use than other families.[10]

Murray Straus, in a study of a sample of university students in 1969 (already referred to on page 47), found no differences in parents' use of physical punishment amongst college students from middle- and working-class families. He developed a 'linkage theory' suggesting that parents of upwardly mobile college students were using socialisation techniques aimed at preparing their children for the class of destination (the middle class).[11] This theory, in turn, was looked at critically by Suzanne Steinmetz, who suggests that a more sophisticated analysis of parents' occupations produces much clearer linkages than those provided by crude social-class analysis. The sample in her study (referred to on page 47) was small, but the results are interesting. Fathers' occupations were classified according to the sort of demands made on them in their job; students were asked about physical punishment in their home and about the traits which they thought their parents' rated most highly. They also answered a series of questions designed to test whether they were, in general, people with 'closed' or 'open' minds (the 'Rokeach Dogmatism' scale). While social class had no effect, analysis by category of occupation found large differences:

> . . . the *persuasive* category (business executive, salesman) is described by Holland (in another study) as containing individuals who identify with power and strength, and who utilize physical skills and control in interpersonal relationships. It is noteworthy that parents in this category were found to have significantly higher physical punishment scores. Those individuals who are categorized as belonging to the *motoric* environment (e.g. dentists, truck drivers) prefer concrete methods of problem-solving, using physical skills and strength, but are not dominating; and they avoid inter-personal relations. Thus, although they received the next highest physical punishment score, it is considerably lower than the mean score for parents in the *persuasive* category. Individuals who are in the *supportive* (e.g. school teachers, social workers) and *conforming* (e.g. accountants, clerks), environments prefer concrete methods of problem-solving, utilizing verbal skills rather than physical skills and strength. Parents in both these environments have considerably lower punishment scores.

While the categorisation of occupations may seem puzzling, the links with physical punishment are compelling.[12]

## Physical Punishment Rates in Other Countries

### United States of America

In the United States, the most recent research on how often American parents hit their children is described in a report from the Family Violence Research Program at the University of New Hampshire. A 1985 survey of a representative sample of 3,232 families with children under 17 revealed that 90 per cent of parents reported hitting their 3-year-old child during the previous year (the proportion in a

comparable 1975 study was 97 per cent). And, at the other end of the
age-range, about a third (340 per 1,000) of 15- to 17-year-olds were hit
by their parents during the year of the study. The survey also used two
alternative measures of child abuse. The authors of the report,
Murray Straus and Richard Gelles, write: 'What constitutes abuse is,
to a considerable extent, a matter of social norms. Spanking or
slapping a child, or even hitting a child with an object such as stick,
hair-brush or belt is not "abuse" according to either the legal or
informal norms of American society, although it is in Sweden and
several other countries.' So, in measuring the extent of serious
violence by parents against their children, the report gives two figures
– one including all acts of violence in the 'Severe Violence Index'
(kicking, biting, punching, hitting with an object, beating up, burning
or scalding, threatening or using a knife or gun), and the other
omitting hitting with an object. In 1985 the rate (not including 'hitting
with an object') of parental abuse against American children aged
0–17 was 23 per 1,000. 'If this rate is correct, it means a minimum of
1.5 million American children are seriously assaulted each year . . .
The actual rate and the actual number is almost certainly greater
because not all parents were willing to tell us about instances in which
they kicked or punched a child.' If 'hitting with an object' is included,
then 110 out of every 1,000 children were abused which, when applied
to the total of 63 million children living in the United States in 1985,
gives an estimate of 6.9 million physically abused children per year. In
the specific age-range of 15- to 17-year-olds, the survey reveals a rate
of 70 out of 1,000 young people being seriously assaulted – including
'hit with an object' – in the year.

The report covers violence by, as well as to, children in families,
using data from a 1975/76 survey. It reveals that children are the most
violent people of all in American families. The rates are extremely
high for violence against a sibling – 800 out of 1,000 had hit a brother
or sister, and more than half had engaged in one of the acts in the
'Severe Violence Index'. The authors write:

> This came as a surprise, even though it should not have. Had we
> analyzed the issue theoretically beforehand, it would have been
> an obvious prediction because of the well-known tendency for
> children to imitate and exaggerate the behavioural patterns of
> parents, and because there are implicit norms that permit
> violence between siblings, exemplified by phrases such as 'kids
> will fight'.

Even among 15- to 17-year-olds violence against siblings is common: two-thirds had assaulted a sibling at least once in the year, and over a third of these were serious assaults. The rate of violence against parents by their children is much lower – 90 per 1,000 children severely assaulted a parent during the year of the study.

At the end of their report, summarising violence by adult and child members of American families, the authors conclude: 'American society still has a long way to go before a typical citizen is as safe in his or her own home as on the street or in a workplace.'[13]

Another recent American study, reported in *Child Abuse and Neglect* in 1988 (see page 26), looked at a sample of 4,695 students who were enrolled in courses at the University of Iowa over a five-year period. Of these, although only 54 per cent reported that 'physical discipline' was used by their parents, 79.9 per cent reported being spanked, 19.9 per cent to being hit other than spanked, 34.7 per cent to being hit with objects, 5.7 per cent to being punched, 1.7 per cent to being 'severely beaten', 5.4 per cent to being kicked, 3 per cent to being choked, 1.2 per cent to being locked in the closet, 12.1 per cent to being injured by their parents (injuries including bruising – 55 per cent; broken bones – 7 per cent; burns – 8 per cent; head injuries – 11 per cent; etc.) and 1.9 per cent to having received medical services due to discipline by their parents (these medical services included casts, sutures and hospitalisation).[14]

In *Behind Closed Doors*, authors Murray Straus, Richard Gelles and Suzanne Steinmetz write: 'Our results illustrate that most Americans view spanking and slapping a 12-year-old as necessary, normal and good. Seventy per cent viewed slapping or spanking a 12-year-old as somehow necessary; 77 per cent felt this was normal; and 71 per cent viewed these acts as good.' Surprisingly perhaps, and certainly depressingly, the authors found that 'younger Americans are much more likely to view slaps and spankings as necessary, normal and good. The most agreement with these forms of violence . . . came from those under 30. On the other hand less than two thirds of the people we interviewed who were over 50 years of age saw slaps and spankings of 12-year-olds as being necessary, normal and good.' They also found that younger children 'are not only more likely to be struck by their parents, they are more likely to be hit frequently. The youngest children in our survey (three to five year olds) were pushed, grabbed, shoved, slapped, spanked and hit with an object more frequently than older children.' Children under 5 and older teenage children were the most likely to experience violence which held a high chance of causing physical injury – 6.7 per cent of 3- and 4-year-olds and 4.3 per cent of 15- to 17-year-olds had parents use 'dangerous forms of violence' on them during the year in which the study was carried out.[15]

Richard Gelles and Murray Straus have compared the rates of family violence, as measured in two substantial studies in 1975/76 and 1985. They found a startling 47 per cent decrease in the rates of serious physical child abuse (children who are kicked, punched, bitten, beaten up or attacked with a knife or gun) over the period. They put this down to the intense educational campaign and other activities which were designed to combat child abuse. These may have led either to a reluctance to report child abuse or to a reduction in its incidence, or both. They found, however, only small and insignificant reductions in the rates of physical punishment (including hitting children with implements), and comment: 'Not only has physical punishment of children not been a focus of a public effort, but most Americans consider it morally correct to hit a child who mis-behaves.'[16]

Further evidence of the social acceptability of corporal punishment in the United States is shown in the education system. As of February 1989, only 12 American states out of 50 have abolished school corporal punishment, normally administered in America with a wooden 'paddle'; Texas heads the league table of states 'paddling' the most students each year with a figure of 260,386 instances.[17] Over a million incidents of school corporal punishment were reported in the 1986/87 school year, 10,000 to 20,000 students sustaining medical injuries due to this institutionalised form of physical punishment.[18]

## Australia

A 1987 study of Australian mothers' and fathers' punishment methods relied, unusually, on reports from children in primary and secondary school. At primary level, 81 per cent of boys and 74 per cent of girls reported that their mother had hit them, and 76 per cent and 63 per cent that their father had. In secondary school, the percentages dropped considerably, and fathers overtook mothers as the punishers: 14 per cent of boys and 17 per cent of girls were hit by their mothers, and 30 per cent of boys and 22 per cent of girls by their fathers. (Well over 80 per cent of mothers and and fathers were reported as yelling at children in both age-groups.)[19]

In February 1988 the Australian Government Office of the Status of Women published a report on *Community Attitudes Towards Domestic Violence in Australia*, the results of a national survey using a

random national sample. Overall, nearly half the population personally knew either a perpetrator or a victim of domestic violence. Other
findings were as follows:

> 70 per cent see children as most at risk from domestic violence,
> and about half see women as most at risk; violent actions against
> children are much less likely to be classed as domestic violence –
> threatening to hit or actually slapping or smacking a child are
> considered violence by only half the community; about six in ten
> people think that it can be justified for a parent to threaten to hit
> or to slap or smack a child; the more extreme forms of violence
> against children (kicking, beating, threatening or using weapons)
> are considered justifiable by about one in 20 people.

Moreover, a third of the survey sample believed that domestic
violence was a private matter for families, and one in five condoned
the use of physical force by a man against his wife.[20]

## New Zealand

In *Spare the Rod*, Jane and James Ritchie report on two surveys in
1963 and 1977 of child-rearing practices in New Zealand. In 1963,
they write,

> . . . we were surprised by four major features which emerged
> from our data, namely that New Zealand mothers relied on very
> few of the wide range of possible control techniques. Secondly,
> that those they did use were, for the greater part, negative –
> scoldings, growlings, threats, reprimands and physical punish-
> ment. Thirdly, not only did they make infrequent use of positive
> or reward techniques but they had very negative attitudes
> towards these, regarding them as bribes or spoiling and not
> infrequently expecting that good behaviour should be its own
> reward. Finally the emphasis on physical punishment was
> widespread and its effectiveness endorsed by the majority.
> Physical punishment was a moral obligation in, and criterion of,
> good parenting in the sixties. The first principle of parenting was
> 'spare the rod and spoil the child', not 'suffer the little children to
> come unto me.'

The Ritchies suggest that, such was the general acceptance of physical punishment, respondents may have exaggerated their use of it:

This is of course survey data in which respondents notoriously try to present themselves in the best possible light. It may be that these 1963 reports of physical punishment were increased by the naive desire of our respondents to convince us that they took the burdens of parenthood seriously and conscientiously. Parents did not feel bad about the use of physical punishment; few expressed any guilt. In terms of the ideology of punishment, by reporting themselves as punishers, they were putting themselves in the best possible light.

When they repeated the survey 15 years later, they found that

. . . physical punishment persists as the major pillar of parenthood. Indeed, though the percentage of mothers who never use physical punishment has increased from one to 10 per cent, 55 per cent of the mothers in the 1977 re-study now use physical punishment weekly or more compared to 35 per cent 15 years ago. Neither chance nor sampling differences can explain an increase of this magnitude. However, though mothers are now using physical punishment more frequently, they are less likely to regard it as effective. Only 14 per cent of the 1977 group find it unequivocally effective compared to 41 per cent of the earlier sample.

Jane and James Ritchie include fathers as well as mothers in their 1977 survey. Fathers appeared to use roughly the same amount of physical punishment as mothers but, as their contact hours with children were considerably less, their overall rate of punishment per contact hour must be greater. The Ritchies report that 'Almost twice as many fathers (one in four) as mothers say that physical punishment is "unequivocally effective"; another 50 per cent regard it as "quite effective". Fathers feel more morally justified than mothers in using physical punishment since 50 per cent of the men consider that they are doing the right thing compared to 29 per cent of the women.'

In 1979 the Ritchies asked 110 12- and 13-year-olds in a Hamilton intermediate school about family authority and discipline. Forty per cent of the girls were still being smacked by their mothers, and 36 per cent by their fathers; whereas 34 per cent of the boys were still being smacked by their mothers, and 51 per cent by their fathers. A third of the boys and a quarter of the girls were being hit by one parent, or both, once a month or more frequently. The authors comment: '. . . these children are teenagers, well on the way to adulthood, and they are still being hit with considerable regularity in the pattern and in the places where they were hit as children – legs, bottoms, hands. We think that is degrading for all concerned.' Fathers are more likely than mothers to use implements such as straps or sticks: 'Other implements were also used. Some parents just pick up whatever is nearest and start hitting their child with it. The children mentioned such items as hearth brush, shoes, slippers, belts, newspapers, wooden spoons and garden hoses.' (Most of the children also reported that smacking does not in their – important – view work, see page 20.)

One of the Ritchies' own teenage children related the reaction of classmates to a newspaper report of their parents' research findings: ' "You mean your parents don't beat you up?" was the frequent comment of his incredulous 15 and 16 year old peers.' This response was not surprising, as in a sample of parents of children at one Hamilton primary school, for example, 96 per cent of fathers and 89 per cent of mothers agreed with the statement 'that in certain circumstances it is all right for a parent to smack a child'.[21]

In view of the parental attitudes revealed above, it is not surprising that in Australia and New Zealand, as in the United States, school corporal punishment is still proving resistant to abolition. Some states of Australia have outlawed it, but currently (1989) New South Wales is considering reintroducing school beating. If it did so, it would be following the dubious example of Nazi Germany – the only country that has ever brought back school beating after it had been abolished.

## West Germany

In West Germany 80 per cent of parents responding to a survey, reported in 1964, said that they beat their children, 35 per cent with canes.[22] Another poll in the early 1970s indicated that 'up to 60 per cent of parents believe in beating, not slapping or spanking, but beating their children'.[23] Dr Anette Engfer and Professor Klaus Schneewind reported a more detailed survey of the punishment habits of German families to the Third International Conference on Child Abuse and Neglect in 1981. In this survey 570 families with children aged 8 to 14 were interviewed in 1976. Seventy-five per cent of the mothers and 62 per cent of the fathers reported slapping their child's face. Frequent and very frequent slaps were reported by 7 per cent of the mothers and 4 per cent of the fathers (but 7.5 per cent of the children questioned reported being slapped very frequently by their mothers, and 10 per cent by their fathers). Spanking was reported by 40 per cent of the mothers and 36 per cent of the fathers; frequent and very frequent spanking by 1.4 per cent of the mothers and 0.7 per cent of the fathers. (Again, the children's estimates were higher – 3.4 per cent reporting frequent and very frequent spanking by their mother, and 3.2 per cent by their father.) Approximately 10 per cent of the mothers and 8 per cent of the fathers said that they occasionally beat their children with a stick or belt. The authors point to the fact that their sample of parents is not representative. For instance, one-third of the fathers had a university degree, as against 8 per cent in the German population; single parents and families under pronounced stress were under-represented or not included. Thus they believe that the survey in fact underestimates the incidence of physical punishment.[24]

In a new study started in 1982, Dr Engfer found that 16 per cent of parents with very young children used physical punishment 'coming close to abusive behaviour'. And a recent survey of 735 parents for the journal *Eltern* found that around 60 per cent of children of all age-groups received physical punishment, with the highest rates being reported for those aged between 4 and 10.[25]

### Societies in which Children Are Not Hit

There are some societies where there is no tradition of family violence against children. Having studied the literature, Dean Herman reports that it is rare in Japan.[26] However, it should be noted that another commentator, William Goode, indicates that the Japanese child is rarely left alone, is severely restricted, and that teasing and ridicule are the main teaching and disciplinary techniques.[27]

Urie Bronfenbrenner, in *Two Worlds of Childhood: US and USSR*, reports that in the Soviet Union corporal punishment 'is viewed not merely as ineffective but harmful', however 'less cultured parents do on occasion resort to physical punishment'.[28] Jill Korbin, probably the leading expert on cross-cultural studies of child abuse, also found very little child abuse or neglect in China:

> Although the use of physical punishment is strongly disapproved, the Chinese do not claim that parents never resort to spanking their children. Spankings are not severe, however, and apparently do not turn into beatings. Visitors to China repeatedly report that it is rare to see children crying or parents scolding or hitting

their children . . . Spankings are seen by the Chinese as arising from parental frustration that overtakes reason. The strict prohibition of physical punishment in the schools reflects the belief that spanking or physical sanctions are not effective methods for changing children's behaviour.[29]

David Levinson's cross-cultural study of 46 small-scale societies ('a distinct cultural unit with no indigenous written language') and 'folk societies' ('whose members share a common cultural tradition, produce at least 50 per cent of their own food, and are under the political control of a larger nation-state') reported the following findings in 1981. Physical punishment of children was 'common' in only 4 per cent of these societies, 'frequent' in 22 per cent, 'infrequent' in 37 per cent and 'rare' in 37 per cent. Twenty-one of the 34 societies reporting 'rare' physical punishment are societies with extended or polygynous family households. The author comments:

The extended or polygynous family household–low physical punishment linkage most likely reflects the presence of alternative caretakers in the household who share child rearing responsibilities. Second, the inclusion in the sample of a number of hunting and gathering societies with nuclear family households such as the Copper Eskimo or Ona: in these type of societies too children are rarely treated harshly.[30]

This finding supported a previous study, reported in 1971, which had found that harsh disciplinary techniques tend to be absent in small-scale societies.[31]

By 1989 children in Sweden, Finland, Denmark, Norway and Austria were protected by a comprehensive prohibition of physical punishment. As the next chapter shows, these legal reforms, together with public education, have already led to dramatic changes of attitude and practice among parents, and already one never sees children being hit in public. But it will probably be some time, even in those countries, before hitting a child becomes as rare an occurrence as hitting other people.

# CHAPTER 3

# BANNING PHYSICAL PUNISHMENT: THE SCANDINAVIAN EXPERIENCE

*'Children are entitled to care, security and a good upbringing. Children are to be treated with respect for their person and individuality and may not be subjected to corporal punishment or any other humiliating treatment.'*
(Swedish Parenthood and Guardianship Code)

When the Children's Legal Centre wrote to the Secretary of State for Social Services early in 1988, proposing that the department should establish a public education campaign to dissuade parents from hitting their children, the then junior health minister, Edwina Currie, replied: 'The Government consider that existing legislation adequately protects children from parental assault and that a law prohibiting corporal punishment in the domestic home would be both unrealistic and unworkable, however stringent or comprehensive the legislation.'[1]

Yet just across the North Sea in Scandinavia, more than 4 million children are now legally protected from all physical punishment – slapping, smacking, beating, etc. – by their parents or anyone else, in their homes and outside them. Four countries – Sweden, Finland, Denmark and Norway – have taken the lead in insisting on children's rights to non-violent methods of child-rearing. In March 1989 they were joined by Austria.

Sweden became the first country to add a specific ban on physical punishment of children to its civil law during 1979 – the International Year of the Child. But the first official moves to discourage the hitting of children had been taken in the 1960s. In February 1982 the Nordic Council discussed and agreed a recommendation which urged its five member countries 'to introduce similar legal regulations prohibiting the use of corporal punishment or any other abusive treatment of children'. Now, in 1989, it appears that current legal reforms in

Iceland, the fifth member of the Council, may shortly see that recommendation fulfilled.[2]

Outside Scandinavia and Austria, it appears there has, as yet, been little progress to limit parents' rights to hit children in Europe, despite a Council of Europe Committee of Ministers recommendation in 1985 which proposed that all member states should 'review their legislation on the power to punish children in order to limit or indeed prohibit corporal punishment, even if violation of such a prohibition does not necessarily entail a criminal penalty'.[3] In Switzerland the explicit confirmation of parents' punishment rights was deleted from the Civil Code in 1978, but a commentary from the Swiss Federal Council to the Federal Assembly indicated that this was not a significant reform: 'Parental authority also includes the right to inflict punishment on the child to the extent necessary for its education. This right does not, however, require special mention in law. The French Civil Code and the Italian Civil Code omit it.'[4] The deletion appears to have no effect on Swiss parents' rights. Changes in the Swiss Criminal Code have been implemented to ensure protection for children against, in the words of the Federal Council, 'repeated, quasi-habitual or systematic beatings' which 'are evidently abuses of the right of chastisement even if they do not immediately result in visibly deleterious effects'. Some even argued against these changes, and wanted parents' rights to use physical punishment expressly mentioned in the code.[5]

A report from Austria to a European colloquy on violence in the family, held in November 1987, suggested that

> . . . under Austrian law corporal punishment is illegal both for parents and teachers . . . Austrian law has developed in such a way that no differentiation is made any longer between 'legitimate' maltreatment, i.e. which does not lead to physical injuries, and 'illegitimate' maltreatment followed by injuries; the new law specifically prohibits all and any kinds of child abuse.

The report refers to a new Penal Code which came into force on 1 January 1975: 'Of importance is that these provisions are no longer based on special rules resulting from parental power, but that they specifically refer to persons in need of protection and, at the same time provide special protection under the criminal law.'[6] In March 1989, the Austrian Parliament agreed unanimously to add a clear prohibition on the physical punishment of children to its family law and Youth Welfare Act to ensure that there can be no confusion. This states that 'using violence and inflicting physical or mental suffering is unlawful' in bringing up children.

In the four Scandinavian countries, the legal reforms have been clear and explicit. In each country the purpose of legal change has been primarily educational – asserting that it is simply not acceptable to hit children and emphasising the potential dangers of all physical punishment. The changes are to civil not criminal codes; they carry no penalties and do not directly affect the criminal law which outlaws assault in each country.

The reforms have undoubtedly removed the confusion which previously existed in all these countries as to whether hitting children was acceptable and legal, or not. There is no doubt that the changes, together with the interest and debate they have provoked and the public education that has generally accompanied them, have already changed parents' attitudes significantly, even dramatically, towards non-violent child-rearing.

While there was little parliamentary opposition to the changes, public opinion, at least in some of the countries, did not favour the reforms when they were proposed. In Denmark, for example, a poll in 1970 showed that only 25 per cent of respondents supported a ban, and that almost 70 per cent were against it.[7]

The research director of a large-scale project looking at 'Childhood, Society and Development' in the five Nordic countries, Lars Dencik, comments: 'There is no doubt in my mind that over the last decade a dramatic change in parental attitudes has taken place in the Scandinavian countries . . . Although our project has not particularly focussed on parental physical punishment, we do indeed see very little if anything at all of that in the upbringing of the children we study.' Professor Dencik suggests that only in Finland and Iceland 'which have undergone the most rapid urbanization and social transformation' have the researchers noted tendencies 'of what could perhaps best be labelled a "cultural lag" in some sectors of the population – mostly newly-urbanized working class parents. In these sectors, the ideology of negotiating with their children and abstaining from physical punishment is perhaps less pronounced than what otherwise nowadays seems to be the rule among Scandinavian parents.'[8]

Scandinavian countries are undoubtedly very much more child-centred than the UK, but that has been a conscious and planned development from an equally unpromising start. Standards of family support and state-provided child care are enviable. Attempts to reduce violence have extended to voluntary agreements not to promote war toys, and action which has dramatically reduced child accidents. Some sections of the British press tend to caricature Swedish society as a bureaucratic nightmare of socialist state intervention. Thus, in December 1988, when the debate on introducing an anti-smacking law in England and Wales hit the press, some favourite myths about the numbers of Swedish children who are taken into care were trotted out by columnists defending smacking, and a Member of Parliament. Mary Kenny, writing in the *Daily Mail*, suggested that Sweden's legal reform had led 'not only to 25,000 children being forcibly removed from their parents' care, but to a tell-tale culture where the family is spied upon and denounced, sometimes for malicious reasons, by other parties'.[9]

In fact, there is no evidence whatsoever that the Swedish anti-smacking law has had any effect on state intervention in families. On the contrary, the general trend in Sweden (and the rest of Scandinavia) is to lower rates of compulsory intervention and care. Compared with England and Wales, the proportion of the child population in care away from home is lower (see page 86), and the proportion of those in care who are living in institutions rather than foster families is tiny. If Scandinavia's experience is to be brought into the domestic debate on hitting children, as it should be, it would be good if commentators could be persuaded to check their facts.

## Sweden

In Sweden moves to make hitting children unacceptable and ultimately illegal began a long time ago. The traditional right of the (male) head of the household to beat his wife, servants and children was first limited in 1864, when a new penal code ended legalised wife-beating. A few decades later, servants were also protected, but criminal and family law continued to confirm parents' rights to physically punish their children. Tor Sverne – a judge who, as first chairman of the Children's Rights Commission, played a central role in the Swedish reforms – states that, at the beginning of this century, children were regarded as their parents' property:

> They had to obey without protest, they had to help their parents with all sorts of things and they were very often forced to go out and work at a very early age. What parents said was always right and the will of the child was – as one said in Sweden – sitting in the birch. It was regarded as self-evident that parents and other carers had not only the right but also the duty to chastise the

child, if it did not obey. When our first family legislation was passed about 1920 it was therefore logical to state explicitly that parents were entitled to chastise their children, if they did not obey.[10]

In 1949, when a Parenthood and Guardianship Code was introduced, the word 'punish' was replaced by 'reprimand', and there was some discussion of the need to discourage more severe forms of physical punishment. In 1957 the provision in the criminal law on assault, which excused parents who caused minor injuries through physical punishment, was removed. At the same time corporal punishment was formally prohibited in Swedish schools, coming into effect in 1958. In 1960 it was abolished in all other child care institutions.

The debate continued – partly because of a number of cases of child abuse in which parents claimed they were exercising their right to chastise their child. Most agreed that corporal punishment should be avoided, but some felt it would be going too far to ban it altogether. So in 1966 a further legal reform deleted the provision allowing 'reprimands' from the Parenthood and Guardianship Code. Thus from 1966 Swedish law no longer gave parents the right to hit their children – but nor was there any explicit ban on all physical punishment. In 1975, therefore, it was still possible for a Swedish municipal court to acquit a father accused of maltreating his 3-year-old daughter, who had been brought to hospital with red blisters all over her body, on the grounds that he had not been proved to have exceeded 'the right of corporal chastisement that a guardian has towards a child in his custody'.

An information campaign to discourage the use of corporal punishment was launched with government funds in 1972, following a survey which showed that only about 60 per cent of the population knew that it was not legal.[11]

Then five years later, in 1977, the Riksdag (Swedish Parliament) set up a Children's Rights Commission. This multi-disciplinary committee – initially chaired by Tor Sverne, then a senior district judge – includes lawyers, psychologists and psychiatrists, representatives of official and voluntary bodies and some politicians. One of its first tasks, proposed by Tor Sverne, was to investigate the feasibility of inserting an explicit ban on all physical punishment into the Parenthood and Guardianship Code. Its first report, *The Child's Right: 1 A Prohibition against Beating*, was presented to the government in Autumn 1977 and unanimously recommended that 'an explicit ban on subjecting children to physical punishment or other degrading treatment should be introduced into the Parenthood and Guardianship Code'. The report included a draft Bill.[12]

The Children's Rights Commission argued that there was already such a ban in education legislation and in the constitution for child care institutions:

The Commission holds that the same concept should be expressed in the Parenthood and Guardianship Code. The proposal would mean stating explicitly that children may not be punished by means of blows, beatings, boxing the ears, and by other similar means, and that children may not, for any other reason or cause, be subjected to acts of physical or mental coercion.

The Commission maintains that physical punishment is a form of degrading treatment; mentally humiliating and dismissive treatment is another. Their effect can be identical, that is to say, lack of self-esteem, and a personality change which may leave its mark on the child throughout its childhood and adolescence, and which may affect it as an adult. Even mild physical reprimands should be avoided in the opinion of the Commission because:

The primary purpose of the provision is to make it clear that beating children is not permitted. In fact, there are many who are unaware that it is not permitted. Secondly, the Commission wishes to create a basis for general information and education for parents as to the importance of giving children good care and as to one of the prime requirements of their care. The proposed provision should, in the long term, contribute towards reducing the number of cases of acts of physical violence on children.

Child psychologists and child psychiatrists have long agreed that it is improper to punish children physically, and that physical violence may cause physical as well as mental injury. If the carer accepts violence and uses it on the child, the risk exists that the child will also use violence in the future in order to achieve its ends.

In conclusion, the Commission stresses the importance of the public being informed that it is not permitted to beat children for the purpose of caring for them, and of a recurrent general parent education programme being set up as soon as possible. The Commission mentions in this respect that there are many immigrants in Sweden who come from countries where beating is a part of children's upbringing.

The proposal was sent out for consultation. There was little opposition, and the government introduced a Bill early in 1979 to add the following section to the Parenthood and Guardianship Code: 'The parent or guardian shall exercise necessary supervision in accordance with the child's age and other circumstances. The child may not be subjected to physical punishment or other injurious or humiliating treatment.' Following further reforms of family law in 1983, the section now reads: 'Children are entitled to care, security and a good upbringing. Children are to be treated with respect for their person and individuality and may not be subjected to corporal punishment or any other humiliating treatment.'[13]

All political parties gave the reform their support. A few members of the Riksdag (believed to represent extremist religious sects) opposed the new law on the grounds that it was 'unnecessary and even dangerous', because 'by removing the biblical right of the father to chastise his child, many well-meaning parents would be stamped as criminals and many children would never learn how to behave'. But a Conservative, Sixten Pettersson, argued: 'In a free democracy like our own we use words as arguments not blows. We talk to people not beat them. If we cannot convince our children with words, we shall never convince them with a beating.'

Following the debate in the Riksdag, the Bill was passed by an overwhelming majority of 259 to 6 on 14 March 1979, and the new provision came into force on 1 July – half-way through the International Year of the Child.

On the day that the measure became law, Swedish television reported it prominently. A reporter went to a nursery and asked some five- or six-year-old children whether they thought it was a good law; he got a very enthusiastic chorus of 'yes'. Then he asked: 'Your mother is out one day, and you're left at home. There is some good jam in the kitchen. You think it is so good that you get a spoon and start eating it. What should your mother do when she comes home?' The children replied that their mothers should tell them not to do things like that. 'Well', says the reporter, 'your mother goes out again the next day, and you can't resist the temptation to take some more jam. What should your mother do when she comes home this time? Should she box your ears or something like that?' Watching the programme, Tor Sverne was very anxious as to what the answer to this provocative question would be: 'But they did it well', he says, 'they answered "no"; "But what ought your mother to do then?" asked the reporter. "Lock up the jam", said the children, and I could let my breath out.'

The reform was well publicised in the newspapers as well as on television. 'One could hear people talking about it on their way to and from work, on the buses and so on', says Tor Sverne. There must also have been lively conversations at family breakfast tables, because a short and direct message about the new law was printed on milk cartons, which are often used in Sweden as a vehicle for public information. There is a cartoon of a little girl saying, 'I'll never ever hit my own children', followed by an explanation of the law, and an answer to an 'ordinary confused father' who has tried everything, including beating, to stop his 3-year-old crawling under a fence onto a railway line.[14] The Ministry of Justice invested in a very large-scale education campaign: 600,000 copies of a full-colour, 16-page pamphlet, *Can You Bring Up Children Successfully without Smacking and Spanking?*, were distributed to every household with children, to social welfare and child health centres, and so on. The pamphlet was also translated, in slightly shortened form, into 10 minority languages spoken by immigrants to Sweden, including English, Arabic and Finnish.[15]

It emphasises that 'while the purpose of the new legislation is indeed to make it quite clear that spanking and beating are no longer allowed, it does not aim at having more parents punished than hitherto'. Under the headline, 'The law says no to physical punishment', the pamphlet goes on to explain that

> Psychologists, psychiatrists and other people whose work gives them an insight into the parent–child relationship are practically unanimous in agreeing that all forms of physical punishment are highly objectionable as a method of bringing up children. A parent who strikes his or her child is not going to gain anything positive in the way of child education by this act – rather, the child runs the risk of suffering some form of mental harm.
>
> The law therefore now forbids all forms of physical punishment of children, including smacking, etc., although it goes without saying that you can still snatch a child away from a hot stove or open window if there is a risk of its injuring itself.
>
> Should physical chastisement meted out to a child cause bodily injury or pain which is more than of very temporary duration it is classified as assault and is an offence punishable under the Criminal Code. In theory at least, this was also true

before the new Bill came into force, although it was not generally known. However, the advent of the new law has now swept all doubt aside, although as before trivial offences will remain unpunished, either because they cannot be classified as assault or because an action is not brought.

The pamphlet emphasises that many psychological punishments are at least as bad for a child's development as beating: as examples it gives threatening, scaring, ridiculing or ostracising, including not speaking to a child for several days, or locking a child up. Such actions as these, which constitute 'injurious or humiliating treatment', are also forbidden.

In an historical section, the pamphlet indicates that both the Church and the law had strongly supported the physical punishment of children:

Even as recently as the beginning of the 20th century most people held the view that children should obey their parents and other authorities without question, displaying an insistence on discipline which found its counterpart in many other areas of society. Hand in hand with this unconditional obedience demanded of children went a need for punishments of various kinds, for it was generally never realized that there were considerable risks associated with this method of bringing up children.

A bishop, in a seventeenth-century commentary on the catechism, stressed the view that 'true paternal love lies in a sensible use of the birch upon one's children'.

In another section of the pamphlet, a member of the Children's Rights Commission, Gunnel Linde, gives her views on why the law has been passed:

Because it is a natural historical development. We have already done away with the right to beat one's wife and servants. We have done away with the right to strike children at school.

Because our democratic community needs children taught to think for themselves, who are used to making their own choices and to shouldering responsibility. It is impossible to beat a child into obedience and at the same time expect it to be able to think for itself.

Because bringing up a child is much easier if you do not resort to beating. Children want to like you so very much it is a pity to destroy a feeling of kinship and mutual understanding by beating if it can be avoided. You don't go round hitting your friends, do you? Why should you hit your children then?

Gunnel Linde – who is also currently the chairwoman of the Swedish voluntary organisation, BRIS (Barnens Ratt I Samhallet – Children's Rights in Society) – believes that, in the long run, the legal prohibition must lead to fewer cases of child abuse: 'By making the law stress that the aim was to make it possible to raise children without violence, we made the community at large share some of the responsibility for its achievement, and so the community must help. We must build up a programme of preventive measures and introduce the concept of parent training.'

Schools were another obvious target for education about the new law. As Tor Sverne informed the author, the Bill was very short,

> . . . but has a content which concerns everybody. So we thought it would be a good Bill to use as an example in schools when teaching pupils how a Bill is made. A summary was written of everything that happened before it was passed. The reader is told why a Commission for Children's Rights was appointed, what the Commission proposed, what was said when the proposal was circulated for comment, the government's proposal, what was said in Parliament and in conclusion the Bill itself is presented. In this way Swedish pupils will learn firstly how a bill is made and secondly what this particular Bill says about corporal punishment.

Professor Adrienne Haeuser of the University of Wisconsin, Milwaukee, who visited Sweden in 1981 and 1988 to assess the effectiveness of the new law, found that in 1988 'the law continues to be discussed in parent education classes which are available to all expectant parents, in child health clinics used by "99.99 per cent" of all parents, and as appropriate in the public health nurse's [equivalent of health visitor] mandatory home visit during a baby's first month. It may also be discussed in the mandatory health screening of all four-year-olds.'

In the school system, Professor Haeuser found that the law and suggestions for class discussion appear in the National School Administration's 9th Grade (roughly 13-year-olds) 'Lesson plan on Child Development'. In compulsory English-language lessons, one proposed exercise focuses on attitudes to physical punishment of children as a tool for expanding pupils' English vocabulary and syntax. The exercise includes an audio-tape, *Spank Them – Don't Spoil Them*, presenting a conversation in which an English man and woman defend physical punishment, while another woman without an English accent clearly disagrees.[16] The Englishman says: 'My father beat me when I did something wrong. I do the same to my boys. Always have done, since they were small. But they know I love them and I do it because I love them. I want them to grow up knowing what's right and what's wrong. I do it for them.' The Englishwoman, Fiona, says she would never use a stick, but she does smack her children sometimes: 'Quite often I suppose, but not that hard. It's usually when I'm tired or angry or something like that. But if you ask me it doesn't do much good. Well, what I mean is, it might make me feel better but it often makes them worse. I sometimes wonder if it doesn't make them more aggressive.' The other woman agrees: 'Exactly! And the more you hit them, the more they'll hit others. That's where violence starts. It's not just on the television, it's at home. Anyway, it's not right. It's unfair because there are two standards: if grown-ups are allowed to hit children, why shouldn't children be allowed to hit grown ups . . .?'

The dialogue gets heated and ends with the Englishman saying: 'You women are really being naïve and sentimental. Now what I say is spank them, don't spoil them. And believe me . . . if you ever have any children of your own, I think you'll find that is very good advice.' The second woman responds: 'Never! I think your ideas are horrible and dangerous and if I do ever have any children of my own, I'll never let you near them.'

Swedish children are thus being given a bonus lesson in prevailing English cultural attitudes, along with their English-language learning.

The fact that 1979 was the International Year of the Child provided a context for the new law to be promoted world-wide as well as internally. Rädda Barnen (the Swedish Save the Children Federation) organised an international seminar in Geneva in 1980 to explain the reform and 'to make an initial assessment of the extent to which this experience could constitute a spearhead for international action in the children's rights field'. As already quoted, Bertil Ekdahl from the Swedish Ministry of Justice explained why the law had been changed:

> Maltreatment of a child is an evil, and its incidence is difficult to reduce. However . . . one way can be to convince parents to avoid physical punishment. Of course, light chastisement is far from

being maltreatment, but there are still great risks that the parent who is used to chastising his child will gradually increase the degree of violence and, one day, will beat the child badly. Most parents who are prosecuted for maltreating their children defend themselves by saying 'I didn't mean to hurt him, I just administered physical punishment which I am entitled to do.' As long as it is not totally clear that a parent may not use physical violence when bringing up a child, it will be difficult to stop or reduce child assault.

But, in addition to the links with child abuse, there was the basic human rights argument: 'By the prohibition of physical punishment, the legislator wanted to show that a child is an independent individual who can demand full respect for his or her person, and who should thus have the same protection against physical punishment or violence as we adults see as being totally natural for ourselves.'[17]

Tor Sverne, when speaking about the ban on physical punishment to various Swedish and international audiences, has found it necessary to make some general points. First, that there is a clear line between physical punishment and physical intervention to avert danger:

It is of course necessary to use physical force to stop a child running out into a street with very busy traffic. It is not this that is forbidden . . . I have many a time been told that it is necessary to smack a small child on its fingers when the child is going to put a steel wire or something like that into the electric socket. I don't believe this. I am not convinced that the parents will gain their end by rapping the child on its knuckles. There is more likely to be a risk that the child will be curious about why it can't do this, and the child may then try to do it again when the parents aren't looking.

He advises parents either to buy safe electrical fittings, or to keep their children away from this sort of danger.

Secondly, concerning hitting older children, his experience as a judge leads him to believe that 'few children have had as much physical chastisement at home as those who are convicted of crimes. Evidently, chastisement has not resulted in their acceptance of the rules of society later on' (see page 43).

Thirdly, the new law does not imply that children should decide everything for themselves, and be allowed 'to behave wildly or be left to drift'. There must be supervision and limits. He accepts that this means that more is being demanded of parents: 'The method of bringing up children by talking sense to them and so on requires both time and patience on the part of parents.'

Finally, it is also important to emphasise that the ban

> . . . does not mean we must constantly keep ourselves under control. Of course we don't want to have a society where everyone is suffering from highly strung nerves because they never have an outlet for their feelings. No it is better if we sometimes forget ourselves and misbehave. But it is important if this happens that we realize what we have done afterwards and that we confess that we have acted wrongly. Generally – at least I hope so – we can admit that we are in the wrong when other adults are concerned, but it seems to be much more difficult for us to do it when we have treated children in a wrong way.
>
> I think there is much to be gained if we could change that attitude.[18]

In Sweden itself there was little parliamentary opposition to the new law, but there were, of course, some groups and some individual parents who were opposed to it. The only serious challenge in 1979 was mounted by seven parent members of a Protestant Free Church congregation in Stockholm – three couples and a divorcee with children aged between 20 months and 12 years. They made an application to the European Commission of Human Rights shortly after the new law was implemented, alleging that the legislation breached rights guaranteed to them by the European Human Rights Convention, including the right to respect for family life. The parents' case, summarised in the commission's report, was that they believed in 'traditional' ways of bringing up their children, 'and in particular, as an aspect of their religious doctrine, they believed in the necessity of physical punishment of their children, which they justify by reference to Biblical texts and doctrinal works . . .'. The applicants complained that the state of Swedish law resulting from the introduction of the 1979 legislation

> . . . makes the corporal punishment and humiliating treatment of children by their parents a criminal offence to the same extent as if such acts were committed against strangers. They maintain that this state of the law violates their rights to respect for family life, to freedom of religion and to respect for their rights to

ensure that their children's education and teaching is in conformity with their own religious and philosophical convictions.

The Swedish government contended that the amendment to the
Parenthood and Guardianship Code was 'an incomplete law'. It has
no accompanying sanction and has not affected, either directly or
indirectly, the scope or interpretation of Swedish criminal law. It
argued that only by the complete prohibition of all corporal
punishment could criminal acts of violence against children be
effectively discouraged. The amendment of the code 'was intended to
encourage a reappraisal of the corporal punishment of children in
order to discourage abuse'. Its underlying purpose was to 'strengthen
the rights of children and encourage respect for them as individuals' –
a humanitarian objective 'best pursued by way of a general policy of
education in its broadest sense'.

The commission rejected the parents' case and in its decision
declaring the application 'inadmissible', released on 13 May 1982, it
accepted the government's arguments, concluding that 'the actual
effects of the law are to encourage a positive review of the punishment
of children by their parents, to discourage abuse and prevent excesses
which could properly be described as violence against children'. The
commission described the Swedish criminal law on assault as 'a
normal measure for the control of violence, and that its extension to
apply to the ordinary physical chastisement of children by their
parents is intended to protect potentially weak and vulnerable
members of society'. The official summary of the decision stated:

> The existence of legislation prohibiting all corporal punishment
> of children, but which does not provide for any sanctions in this
> respect, cannot be considered as an interference in the exercise of
> the parents' right to respect for family life. Neither does the fact
> that corporal punishment of a child by his parents may expose
> the latter to criminal prosecution for assault, by the same
> standards as assault of a person outside the family, constitute an
> interference with the exercise of this right.[19]

Thus the European human rights machinery has judged that laws
such as Sweden's are justified; and that the state can legitimately
interfere in family life with the objective of promoting children's
rights and protecting them from violence in this way.

During a brief visit to Stockholm early in 1989, I found unanimity amongst people in the street, government officials, legal observers, academics, and so on, that everyone knew about the law – and, in particular, every child knew and was quick to remind their parents of it. People who had doubted its effectiveness in 1979 felt that, in practice, it had had a dramatic effect on attitudes to children and to violence. Nobody in Sweden claimed any longer that physical punishment 'didn't do *me* any harm'. Nobody would be seen in public hitting a child. A worker at BRIS[20] suggested that in the privacy of the family home there was undoubtedly still some physical punishment, but if children felt aggrieved, they would at least know the law.

In terms of legal action there has been no rush by children to drag their parents through the courts. It appears there has been just one prosecution in 10 years which would probably not have taken place before the 1979 reform. In 1984 an 11-year-old boy reported his father to the police for 'spanking' him, and the father was fined a nominal 100 Swedish kronor (about £9) for assault under the criminal law. This was reported widely in the Swedish media and even led to comment in some English newspapers.[21] It seems clear that if there had been other similar prosecutions, they would be well known.

A decision of the Swedish Supreme Court in December 1988 showed that the determination to maintain a clear principle of opposition to the use of physical coercion has been maintained. During an incident at a school, in October 1986, a teacher broke up a fight and asked the boys involved to follow him to the office. One 15-year-old refused, saying he had not been involved. The teacher grabbed him by the neck; the boy ducked out but was grabbed again. The force used was not sufficient to cause bruises, but it was painful and caused some redness on the skin. The boy and his parents went to the police, and prosecution followed. The Supreme Court decision was that the teacher was guilty, as the force used was not in self-defence, but the teacher was not in fact punished.[22]

The only current discussion of the issue in Sweden is caused by a small fundamentalist religious group, Maranata, which preaches the literal interpretation of the Bible and encourages parents to use physical punishment. Early in 1989 its leader, Arne Imsen, was fined for exhorting parents on the radio to beat their children.[23]

There has been some formal research assessing the effects of the successive legal changes and public education programmes. The most exciting statistics are those revealing changes in parental attitude. Between 1965 and 1981, public opinion polls commissioned by the Swedish Save the Children Federation (Rädda Barnen), and carried out by the Swedish Institute for Research on Public Opinion, showed a wholesale transformation in parents' attitudes. In 1965, 53 per cent felt that corporal punishment was 'sometimes necessary'. By 1981 this had reduced to 26 per cent (22 per cent of women and 29 per cent of men), and the proportion of parents stating that children should be raised without corporal punishment had doubled from 35 per cent to 71 per cent (74 per cent of women and 68 per cent of men). Over the same period, the proportion in the 'don't know' category had also reduced from 12 per cent to 3 per cent.

Predictably, those who had been physically punished by their parents were more likely to support its use: 41 per cent believing it to be necessary compared with 11 per cent of those who had not been physically punished. Eighty-six per cent of those who had not been physically punished compared with 56 per cent of those that had been, believed parents should manage without physical punishment. The poll revealed that 55 per cent of respondents had been physically punished as children – 49 per cent of them by their parents, 25 per cent by teachers and 7 per cent by other adults. More men (63 per cent) than women (46 per cent) had been physically punished, and older people reported more physical punishment.

The same poll in 1981 revealed that knowledge of the law was more or less universal: 96 per cent knew that physical punishment was forbidden, only 1 per cent believed it was still permitted. The public information campaign had clearly worked. Ten years earlier, in 1971, less than two-thirds of the population knew that physical punishment was illegal and 11 per cent believed that it was permitted.[24] Klaus Ziegert, writing a preliminary report on the Swedish prohibition in 1983, indicates: 'It is unquestionable that the clarity and simplicity of the law itself raised the level of knowledge about it.'[25]

In 1986 a summary of the results of a comparative study of violence towards children in Sweden and the United States by Richard Gelles and Åke Edfeldt was published in *Child Abuse and Neglect*. But as the reported research in Sweden was carried out in 1980, only a year after the new law took effect, and the American figures used in the comparison came from a National Family Violence Survey carried out in 1975, this research can tell us little about the effects of the 1979 ban. Interviews with a representative sample of over 1,000 Swedish families revealed that 27.5 per cent of them had used some form of physical punishment during 1980 (51.2 per cent indicated that they had done so at some point in the past). In the United States, 58.2 per cent of parents (over twice the Swedish percentage) said they had spanked or slapped their child during the year of the survey, and over 70 per cent at some time in the past. Respondents in these two surveys were asked about all kinds of violence to their children, and some form of abuse had been used by 63 per cent of American parents in 1975, and by 29.8 per cent of Swedish parents in 1980. While 13.4 per cent of the American sample reported 'attempting to hit or actually hitting' their child with an object, only 2.4 per cent of Swedish parents reported 'actually hitting' their child with an object. If 'hitting with an object' is left out of the calculation of rates of 'severe violence' towards children in the two countries, then the rates in both are around 4 per cent. Richard Gelles and Åke Edfeldt emphasise that there were a number of methodological differences between the two surveys. They also suggest that the public debate in Sweden may have led Swedish respondents to be more accurate in reporting violence than in the United States where physical punishment is so much more common. There has been no follow-up study since 1980.

The authors of the study find 'stark contrasts' between Sweden and the United States in social attitudes to violence:

While in the US the majority of states permit the corporal punishment of school children, corporal punishment has been outlawed in Sweden since 1958. Legislation prohibiting the spanking of children was passed in 1979 . . . Firearm ownership is also rigorously controlled in Sweden. While nearly half of all American households contain guns, mostly handguns, gun ownership in Sweden is mostly limited to weapons used for hunting. Television violence offers another important contrast. American children witness as many as 15,000 killings each year on television; violent programming in Sweden is severely restricted. (Actually Swedish television is barely on the air as many hours as the average American child watches television in a week.) The level of concern for children's programming in Sweden can be seen in the decision to limit the popular American movie, *ET* to audiences over 11 years of age. A final contrast is in public violence: capital punishment is banned in Sweden, but it is allowed and growing in use and popular support in the US.[26]

Another cross-cultural examination of the use of corporal punishment in Sweden and the United States, reported in *Child Abuse and Neglect* in 1982, concluded:

Frequent research in the US has found that the experience of violence during childhood is inherent in the backgrounds of murderers, assault and batterers, rapists and individuals who commit suicide. It appears that the social ill of violence in society could be most effectively treated by prevention rather than by cure. Changing child-rearing practices might be the single most important action we can take as a society on behalf of today's children, and on behalf of tomorrow's parents. If we can discourage the use of force and encourage the use of open and honest physical affection within the family, this might prove to be a formidable goal and a worthwhile cause.[27]

The largest-scale assessment of the effects of the Swedish ban on physical punishment is that by Professor Adrienne Haeuser mentioned earlier. In 1981, and again in 1988, she conducted extensive interviews with national and local government officials in health, social services and education, and with parents in Stockholm and four other areas of Sweden, with varying populations.[28]

The conclusions, summarised in a 66-page report, are very positive:

Physical punishment is never used on Swedish children in public. Even in the privacy of their homes most Swedish parents do not use even mild physical punishment, that which does not leave injury or more than momentary pain. Instead, to socialize and discipline their children they almost universally resolve conflicts through discussion. This includes stopping unwanted behaviour by immobilizing a child through a firm hold on the child's arms and insisting on eye contact during discussion. Most parents believe it is important to discuss feelings; the child should know the parent is angry and why. Some parents admit the discussion may escalate to yelling, but they believe this is nevertheless more constructive than the humiliation and violence which they believe is inherent in slapping, smacking, spanking, etc.

For pre-verbal infants and toddlers Swedish homes are child-proofed – with public health nurses [health visitors] inspecting and providing child-proofing supplies as necessary – to avoid parent–child conflict.

In 1980 the government-funded National Child Environment Council (Barnmiljörådet) started work in Stockholm, promoting a safe and interesting environment for children.[29]

Professor Haeuser's report continues:

It has apparently become easier for Swedish parents to avoid physical punishment than to defend using it. The 1979 law is now taken for granted in Sweden. Whereas in 1981 parents reported 'thinking twice' before using any physical punishment, in 1988 parents simply said they do not use it. The government has achieved the goal of enabling parents to recognise that even mild physical punishment has the potential of escalating to abuse, and physical punishment is not a constructive childrearing method.

The only parents who sometimes use physical punishment in the privacy of their homes are those under some kind of severe stress for which professional help is needed. Parents who do on occasion resort to a slap, smack or other form of mild physical punishment do not believe physical punishment is useful but use it to relieve their own anger and frustration, and they frequently apologise to their children afterward.

Adrienne Haeuser found that data are not available to determine whether the 1979 law has reduced physical child abuse: 'Most Swedish authorities believe that parents who abuse children have very severe family or other problems which the 1979 law obviously does not address.' Increased sensitivity, however, probably leads to child abuse reports being made earlier, thus facilitating treatment. 'The law has increased child abuse reports by children. However, in the entire country over the nine years of the law only two children have made child abuse reports which were unwarranted.'

She identified only one trend that had changed between the periods of her two visits. In 1981 she felt that permissive child-rearing dominated Swedish family life, and that children were not punished much, physically or otherwise. But by 1988 permissive child-rearing is dead because of changed advice from experts, and an increasingly conservative social and political climate – 'a rather pervasive return to more traditional values and practices in various areas of Swedish life'. She concludes: 'In 1988 parents are imposing rules and limits on children's behaviour, but they are not also resorting to physical punishment.' (Tor Sverne, generally accepting this assessment as did others spoken to during my 1989 visit, pointed out that the ban on physical punishment was, after all, the imposition of 'limits' on adult behaviour; there was a logical connection with imposing limits on children, not a contradiction.)

The end of permissive child-rearing might have had significant implications for parental use of physical punishment: 'One can no longer conjecture that the 1979 law may make little difference in child rearing practices because Swedish parents do not set limits or discipline their children in any event. As of 1988 Swedish parents do appear to be disciplining their children. The miracle is that there has been no serious suggestion of reinstituting physical punishment to achieve this.'

Professor Haeuser believes that the legal reforms and public education in Sweden have stopped the transmission of the use of physical punishment from one generation to the next. Thus while the current generation of children will experience little or no physical punishment, their parents will have received some, and their grand-parents a great deal. She ends by concluding: 'There appears to be no indication that the 1979 law has had any detrimental effects on Swedish children, families or society.'

Finally, given the British tendency to misinterpret Swedish social statistics, it is important to stress that state intervention in family life is not at a high level and is reducing. For example, the total number of children and young people in compulsory care in Sweden on 31 December 1982 was 6,948. The equivalent figure in 1986 was 4,939; this represents 2.7 children per 1,000 of the population aged 0–17.[30] In England, on 31 March 1982, there were 50,467 children in the various forms of compulsory care. The equivalent figure for 1986 was 38,812; this represents 3.5 children per 1,000.[31] The proportion of children in care who are in institutions rather than in foster-care is also very much lower in Sweden.

## Finland

The Finnish Child Custody and Right of Access Act 1983, which came into force on 1 January 1984, sets out some general principles for child-rearing. It begins: 'A child shall be brought up in a spirit of understanding, security and love. He shall not be subdued, corporally punished or otherwise humiliated. His growth towards independence, responsibility and adulthood shall be encouraged, supported and assisted.'

A commentator from the Central Union for Child Welfare in Helsinki suggests that because the ban on corporal punishment formed part of a comprehensive reform of children's law, with an emphasis on children's rights, there was little opposition to the reform. The worries of those who did oppose the change centred around how cases would be proved, and whether it would become a common occurrence for a child to sue a parent for smacking.[32]

As in Sweden, there had been earlier, relevant legal changes.

School corporal punishment was eliminated by the School Order of 8 August 1872. Then, in 1969, an amendment to the Criminal Code on assault removed a provision which stated that a petty assault was not punishable if committed by parents or others exercising their lawful right to chastise a child.[33] (In Finland, this was the only recognition of parents' rights to use physical punishment; family law was silent on the issue.) This amendment left a certain amount of confusion as to whether mild physical punishment was still permitted.

But while in Sweden the next step was a Bill with the sole purpose of prohibiting physical punishment, in Finland a similar reform formed only a small part of a complete overhaul of child custody law.[34] When the Finnish Parliament adopted the Child Custody and Right of Access Act in 1983 there was no controversy in the press or in Parliament. This was probably because a measure that had become highly controversial – a Family Names Bill – was in Parliament at the same time; and while its clauses were carefully scrutinised and voted on, the Child Custody Bill was adopted without a single change, unanimously and practically without debate.

Matti Savolainen of the Ministry of Justice in Helsinki, who was responsible for drafting the 1983 Act, sees its section 1 as using three strategies:

> Firstly the Act attempts to establish certain 'positive' guidelines for the upbringing of the child. Secondly the Act makes it absolutely clear that all violations against the child's integrity (whether 'physical' or 'spiritual') which would constitute a criminal offence if committed by a third person (e.g. assault, unlawful imprisonment, libel, slander, etc.) are equally punishable even when committed by a parent with the intent to discipline the child. And under the Criminal Code even a petty assault committed against a child under 15 is subject to public prosecution when committed by a parent at home. Thirdly the Act explicitly forbids also any degrading treatment ('the child shall not be humiliated') even where such an act would not constitute a criminal offence and even if there are no other direct legal remedies available.[35]

The emphasis of the public information campaign launched by the Ministry of Justice and the National Board of Social Affairs was on positive ways of dealing with parent/child conflicts rather than on the prohibitions. A leaflet entitled *What Is Good Upbringing?* (on a more modest scale than the Swedish one) was available through child health clinics, social welfare offices, and so on.[36]

Similarly, a large-scale campaign launched by the Central Union for Child Welfare, together with the National Boards of Health and Social Affairs, included a leaflet entitled *When You Can't Cope, Find Help: Don't Hit the Child*. Two hundred thousand of these were distributed through the health care and social welfare system, together with 5,000 stickers and 10,000 posters, in the period preceding the implementation of the new law.[37] The leaflet emphasises that children need love and care. It accepts, however, that parents cannot always cope and think of every situation from the child's point of view, and outlines situations in which children may get on parents' nerves. It argues that physical punishment can lead to child abuse when it gets out of control and that, in any case, it harms the child by creating feelings of insecurity and worthlessness. Children need support, encouragement and praise, but also clear, secure limits. Thus parents must be consistent. Life has some basic rules that apply to everyone, and through these the child learns to understand the causes and consequences of behaviour, and to take others into consideration. The leaflet suggests it is inevitable that parents will sometimes feel a failure with their children; small things can make them very angry and they might hit the child. But if this happens, it is important that parents make it clear to themselves what the reasons were: 'Don't defend yourself by speaking about the best interests of the child, or human weakness when you have hurt the child.' Getting information on the different stages of child development will help parents to understand their children better. Conflicts should be sorted out in discussion with the child – but not when the parent is angry. The back page of the leaflet encourages parents to talk about problems, and suggests agencies and individuals whom they can approach. It also encourages anyone who witnesses child abuse to contact child welfare workers at their local social welfare office.

On national television there were also brief spots at peak viewing time before the main evening news programme, both during the preparatory period and as the law came into effect in January 1984. This is a translation of the commentary on one of these:

Do you hit your child?
Is that how you bring him up?
All physical punishment deflates a child's ego. Even a slap makes him or her feel worthless.
A worthless person becomes indifferent.

Through slapping you are raising a bully.
Talk to the child. Settle your differences through discussion.
Make the child party to an agreement. That way you both win.
Decide to deserve your child's respect. As a person.

In Finland, as in Sweden, it appears that everyone, including all children, know about the law. Despite the fact that the police are obliged to bring a prosecution if an assault (including a petty assault) on a child aged under 15 is reported, there have been no cases apart from those involving serious physical abuse.

Public opinion was broadly in favour of the reform in Finland. A poll carried out in autumn 1981 had asked the question: 'After long debate, the physical punishment of children was banned by the Swedish Parliament. In your opinion, should a similar law be passed in Finland too?' 60 per cent felt that there should be a ban, 31 per cent were against it and 9 per cent had no opinion. More women (63 per cent) backed the new law than men (56 per cent), and 72 per cent of respondents aged between 15 and 24 favoured the ban. Reporting the results of this and other relevant polls to the 1982 International Congress on Child Abuse and Neglect in Paris, Finnish researcher Teuvo Peltoniemi concluded that it would be valuable for Finland to adopt similar legislation to Sweden:

There are the good experiences of Sweden's example, and in Finland the population seems to be ready for the change in legislation. This is especially clear when we look at the response from the younger generation. The need for the law is based on the theoretical point of view that the physical punishment of children is just a degree of child battering as well as the empirical evidence which shows how physical punishment often leads to child battering. The difference between the two is very vague. The proposed legislation would clarify the situation and help parents with their responsibilities in raising their children.[38]

Until the 1984 implementation of the Child Custody Act, there was the same confusion in Finland as in other Scandinavian countries, amongst both specialists and the general public, as to whether physical punishment was in fact permitted. In a 1978 survey, 40 per cent of those questioned thought that parents had a legal right to use physical punishment, but over half thought that the right did not exist.[39]

Strong arguments for introducing the new law were to be found in two earlier studies of child abuse cases in Finland. In the first of these, Maija and Martti Santasalo looked at the background of 'battered child' patients in Helsinki Children's Hospital from 1970 to 1976. They found that in the great majority of cases, the perpetrators insisted that they had only used their right to physically punish their child, and they did not consider themselves to have battered their child.[40] In the second study, Marja Korpilahti studied child abuse cases which had been brought before the courts in four Finnish and Swedish cities in the late 1970s. There were only 29 cases, but she noted that every other case had started with physical punishment of the child.[41]

A Finnish Gallup Poll in 1978 found that 69 per cent of Finns had received physical punishment from their parents during their child-hood; the percentage being higher amongst older respondents. Respondents were also asked about their own attitude to parents' use of physical punishment. Fifty-five per cent thought that parents should use other means of solving problems in child-rearing in all situations, while 44 per cent felt that physical punishment was acceptable under some circumstances.

Further polls were carried out in 1981 and 1985, but as the questions used for these were different, no direct comparison can be made with the 1978 results. Between 1981 and 1985, however, there has been a significant drop in support for physical punishment. Respondents (a representative sample of 530 Finns aged over 15) were asked to react to the statement: 'Physical punishment of children is acceptable at least in special situations.' In 1981, 16 per cent 'totally agreed' with the statement; by 1985 this had dropped to 11 per cent. The proportion disagreeing either partly or totally with the statement (i.e. finding physical punishment unacceptable) increased from 44 to 46 per cent, and the proportion of women disagreeing went up from 49 to 55 per cent.[42] Thus, while acceptance of physical punishment remains at a higher level in Finland than in Sweden (where only 26 per cent of the respondents were in favour of it in 1981 – see page 82), there have been positive changes in attitude over a relatively short period.

The results of a large-scale research project, now (1989) being analysed at the Central Union for Child Welfare, will give a clearer picture of the current generation of Finnish children's experience of physical punishment and other forms of abuse, including sexual abuse at home. Pupils in their last year of compulsory schooling (15- and 16-year-olds) were invited to fill in a detailed questionnaire in conditions of privacy during their final school medical check-up;

7,500 completed questionnaires are being analysed. The questions enquire about all forms of violent behaviour by parents (including what the children think are the causes and consequences of physical punishment, and whether they will use such punishment on their own children, if they have any). They are also asked in detail about all forms of sexual harassment and sexual acts with adults. A letter with the questionnaire emphasised the anonymity of the research, explained that the Central Union for Child Welfare was seeking the information in order that appropriate help and advice should be available to young people, and indicated where help could be obtained immediately if wanted. The survey was carried out with the co-operation of health, social welfare and education authorities, and relevant trade unions.[43]

## Denmark

On 1 January 1986, Denmark became the third Nordic country to insist that its 1,355,000 children should be protected from physical punishment. A private Bill (passed by the Danish Parliament on 30 May 1985) added an amendment to the Majority Act stating that 'Parental custody implies the obligation to protect the child against physical and psychological violence and against other harmful treatment'.[44] As in Sweden and Finland, no penalty is attached to the new provision. The Criminal Code makes it an offence to commit violence without provocation or against 'an innocent person', punishable by prison or fines.

Jorgen Graversen, Professor of Law at Aarhus University, writing recently in the *Journal of Family Law* commented:

> The amendment to the Act is more of a manifesto, a notification to parents and others that violence should never be used as a remedy in the upbringing of children. The actual effects of such pedagogical legal provisions are quite uncertain and are, therefore, generally avoided in the Majority Act. Although the provision intended no alteration of the practice of courts in cases of parents' violence towards children, it must be presumed that it will further a development already in progress towards limiting violence permitted towards children.[45]

The Danish reform was carried through despite evidence of strong public opposition: a Gallup Poll in 1984 found that only 25 per cent wanted the formal abolition of parents' right to hit children, while 68 per cent were against abolition. Studies during the 1960s, 1970s and 1980s also showed that about 70 per cent of the Danish population believed that physical punishment, used sparingly, was an important part of child-rearing.[46]

More recently, in 1988, Ole Varming, of the Royal Danish School of Educational Studies in Copenhagen, has looked at the attitudes of a representative sample of 1,000 Danish adults to physical punishment (and other aspects of upbringing). They were asked whether they thought that corporal punishment was necessary for children aged 2 to 3, in response to the following forms of behaviour: 'when they play wildly in spite of repeated warnings'; 'when they fight with siblings'; 'when they persistently refuse to do what parents tell them to'; and 'when they become hysterical'. The adults could respond: 'yes, quite obviously'; 'yes, in certain situations'; 'no, never'; or 'don't know'. A small proportion felt that it was obvious that corporal punishment should be used, rising to 6 per cent in cases of persistent disobedience. A much higher proportion, but in every case under 50 per cent, felt that corporal punishment would be right in certain circumstances, rising to 42 per cent in cases of persistent disobedience. Over half said that corporal punishment should never be used on 2- to 3-year-old children, rising to 69 per cent when the child was 'fighting with siblings'.

The adults were also asked similar questions about the corporal punishment of 5- to 6-year-olds, in response to the child 'taking £2 from your purse without asking'; 'slamming the door'; 'lying'; and 'stealing something worth about £10 from a shop'. The proportion feeling that corporal punishment should obviously be used rose to 16 per cent for stealing from a shop. The proportions believing corporal punishment should never be used remained roughly the same.[47] Ole Varming says that the overall study showed that over half the respondents considered a strict upbringing, aiming at obedience and subordination, to be the correct way to raise children.[48]

Although the Danish population is under a legal duty to tell the local 'social committee' (social services) if they believe a child or young person is exposed to neglect or degrading treatment, there do not appear to be any national statistics of child abuse. Research into cases of child death due to abuse suggests a rate of 0.5 per million inhabitants per year. This accords with figures for Norway and Sweden of 0.4 per million per year, and compares with an estimated figure of 1.7 per million population per year in the United States.[49]

The national report on Denmark presented to the 1987 Council of

Europe Colloquy on Family Violence concludes that, over recent years, there has been mounting consciousness and interest in the problem of violence against children, and in the importance of preventive measures, including public education through booklets and the mass media. The report indicates that studies of families in which children have been exposed to violence identify certain risk groups – amongst them parents 'who were themselves raised strictly, with violence, and so have taken this as their own model for raising children'. And it describes the abolition of the right to hit children as probably 'the most significant initiative at least in the longer view.[50]

Joav Merrick, who worked until recently in the Department of Paediatrics at University Hospital, Copenhagen, has looked at the history of physical punishment and child abuse in Denmark. In 1683 King Christian V provided mothers and fathers with a right in law to strike children and servants with a stick. That this right was put into practice is shown, for example, by Copenhagen's death statistics for 1748: 987 (mostly children) out of 3,328 died because of hitting and beating (see page 5).

In 1866 the law was changed, but parents' rights to punish were not altered, and it was left to the courts to decide the line between physical punishment and child abuse. The right to hit servants had been removed by 1921, and physical punishment in child care institutions and schools was steadily reduced by regulations (for instance, in 1934 specific prohibitions on punishing children for bedwetting, and on cutting their hair as a punishment were introduced). Physical punishment was finally banned in all institutions in Denmark in 1967 (it had been banned in Copenhagen schools in 1952). Joav Merrick reported that the right of parents to hit their children had been challenged by individuals and child welfare organisations over the years before the 1985 reform, and in 1983 the first Scandinavian seminar on Child Abuse and Neglect recommended that the Danish government should join Sweden and Finland in banning parental physical punishment. He expressed his hope that other countries would soon follow the lead of Scandinavia.[51]

## Norway

Norway became the fourth Scandinavian country to ban parental physical punishment in January 1987. News-agency reports led to single-paragraph pieces in several English morning papers the next day: 'Watch it parents – Norway yesterday made corporal punishment of children an offence and gave youngsters the right to report offending parents to the police.'[52]

The wording of the wide provision added to the Parent and Child Act is: 'The child shall not be exposed to physical violence or to treatment which can threaten his physical or mental health.'

Up to 1972, the Norwegian Criminal Code on assault, dating from 1891, stated that parents and others *in loco parentis* had the right to use moderate corporal punishment as part of the upbringing of children. In 1972 that provision was removed, amid a lot of controversy. This caused more rather than less confusion about parents' rights to punish.

In 1981, the Norwegian government became the first country to establish the office of children's ombudsperson (Barneombudet). Målfrid Grude Flekkoy was appointed as the first holder of the office, and is due to retire during 1989 at the end of her second four-year term. Soon after her appointment, a magazine article written by a clergyman and teacher was published and, in the course of answering parents' questions, he advocated 'a good spanking' for a child who would not go to bed. Målfrid Flekkoy went to see the government's legal advisers, as she felt that if this advice was promoting something which was illegal, there should be some intervention. But the response she got only illustrated the confusion that existed following the 1972 change in the Criminal Code.[53]

Then, in 1982, an official committee that had been looking at child abuse and neglect recommended that the law should be changed to ensure that children were not exposed to physical punishment or other humiliating treatment. Its primary reasons for doing so were to influence public opinion and to remove any confusion about the acceptability of physical punishment.[54] This recommendation was referred to the Ministry of Justice. At about the same time, a clergyman appeared on television, saying that he had regularly spanked his six children from the age of 2. Målfrid Flekkoy was on television the next day expressing the general outrage at his viewpoint. A group of lawyers decided to file charges against him. Government legal officers took advice from the ombudsperson and others, and the charges were dropped because of the legal confusion, which had been usefully demonstrated by the incident.

The Ministry of Justice considered the recommendation and produced a report proposing an addition to the Parent and Child Act explicitly prohibiting physical violence and other harmful treatment of children. The report indicated that the 1982 state of the law clearly forbade the use of implements – for example, canes – to punish children, and if a smack with the hand caused bruising or swelling, that too was an offence, but it suggested that spontaneous smacks without injury were still permitted. The ministry indicated that under the current law any harsh physical treatment leading to 'real' pain or involving 'unnecessary' humiliation would not be accepted – but less serious forms of physical punishment would be. The report also quoted a public opinion poll (carried out by an organisation called Scanfact and published in a magazine) which found that 43 per cent were against caning children, 5 per cent believed in it, and 52 per cent felt that it might be necessary in various special circumstances. Previous polls of a sample of the adult population had found that, in 1970, 73 per cent and, in 1978, 60 per cent believed that parents should be able to use moderate physical punishment, such as smacking, slapping, and so on. In 1983, 68 per cent were still against prohibiting all physical punishment.[55]

The Ministry of Justice's proposal went to the Norwegian Cabinet, but was twice shelved by the then Conservative government in 1983 and 1984. The proposal was resurrected when the Social Democrats returned to power in 1985. (The fact that the Prime Minister and 7 out of 17 ministers were women in the new administration could have had something to do with the desire to see the reform through.) When it got to Parliament in 1986, Målfrid Flekkoy spent a lot of time in the corridors and restaurant, lobbying members. In the larger of the two chambers (Odelstinget) of the Norwegian Parliament, the measure was passed with only 3 votes recorded against it (out of a possible 100); in the smaller chamber (Lagtinget) 2 votes were recorded against (out of a possible 50). In the debate in the larger chamber, the Minister of Justice, Helen Bøsterud, suggested that even though parental physical violence was already forbidden in the Criminal Code, the new reform was not superfluous. For many people did not understand or know about the law, and making physical punishment clearly illegal in the Parent and Child Act would inform the general public. There was considerable lack of clarity about parents' rights, and the legal change in 1972 had been just as confusing as clarifying. Now there would be no doubt: in applying the criminal law, the child would have the same protection as everyone else from the use of violence. It was not sufficient only to protect children from 'real' pain and 'unnecessary' humiliation. Physical punishment as a method of bringing up children was no longer acceptable. The Parent and Child Act should contain a comprehensive description of the rights and responsibilities of parents. Other speakers suggested that while the reform might not stop serious abuse, it might stop borderline cases because parents would know what the law said. One of the very few speakers against the reform argued that the law should not be used as a moral text, and asked why children, rather than wives and other potentially threatened groups, should be singled out for a specific prohibition of physical punishment.[56]

There has been very much less public and parent education in Norway about the legal reform and non-violent methods of child-rearing than in Sweden or Finland. But an information campaign on the consequences of physical punishment and other degrading treatment of children was planned by the Ministry of Health and Social Affairs in 1986 and launched early in 1987. A voluntary group, the People's Movement for Children, got funds to print 150,000 copies of booklets promoting the change; one was entitled *I Know I Need Limits, but Do You Need to Knock Them into Me?*[57] There were also newspaper advertisements. Målfrid Flekkoy suggests that the law is well known, and that there has been little controversy since it came into force.

There do not appear to have been any recent assessments in Norway of the prevalence of physical punishment or parents' attitudes to it. Turid Vogt Grinde who was until recently head of the child welfare section of the Norwegian Ministry of Health and Social Affairs comments:

> The general view is that the amount of severe physical punish-
> ment or abuse is low in our quite homogeneous culture. In spite
> of increased awareness, general practitioners and paediatricians
> register few cases of physical abuse. We know less about milder
> forms of punishment. The official non-acceptance of physical
> punishment goes together with general public opinion, but is of
> course no guarantee against misuse in individual families.[58]

Thus in a period of eight years, from 1979 to 1987, four Scandinavian countries have added a total prohibition of all forms of physical punishment and humiliating treatment of children to their law. They have done so as a conscious attempt to improve the status of children and reduce the level of violence in their societies. In March 1989, Austria followed them. Is this the beginning of the end of legalised hitting of children throughout Europe?

# CHAPTER 4

---

# THE LAW AND PHYSICAL PUNISHMENT IN THE UK

*'By the law of England, a parent . . . may for the purpose of correcting what is evil in the child, inflict moderate and reasonable corporal punishment, always, however, with this condition, that it is moderate and reasonable.'*
(Chief Justice Cockburn, *R.* v. *Hopley* [1860])

## Traditional Rights to Hit Children

The law makes a very clear stand against all forms of deliberate physical assault – except hitting children. When it comes to the physical punishment of children, the law draws a protective circle not around the child, but around the punisher. Thus the Children and Young Persons Act 1933, section 1, makes it a criminal offence to 'wilfully assault' or ill-treat a child 'in a manner likely to cause him unnecessary suffering or injury to health'. But the last subsection states: 'Nothing in this section shall be construed as affecting the right of any parent, teacher or other person having the lawful control or charge of a child or young person to administer punishment to him.'

This provision first appeared in the Prevention of Cruelty to and Protection of Children Act 1889 – the first statute to protect children from cruelty. Its wording was adopted following a debate during the Bill's Committee Stage in the House of Commons on 3 July 1889. One member, a Mr Kelly, implied that the instigators of the Bill, the recently formed Society for the Prevention of Cruelty to Children, intended to use it to 'prevent corporal punishment'. He produced a copy of a notice 'in which the Society invites information to be sent to the local secretary by parents and others of all cases of cruelty to children, and the Society undertakes the cost of further inquiry and proceedings'. The government minister said that 'not one single summons has been taken out by the Society against a teacher, and in only one instance was a scholar's expenses paid by the Society'. He was 'anxious to give the teachers an assurance that all reasonable moderate punishment they may have to administer as discipline will not subject them to any liability under the Act'.

As originally drafted, the provision in the 1889 Bill qualified the right to use punishment with the words 'reasonable and moderate', reflecting the common law. But Members of Parliament – whose sole concern was protecting teachers' rights to beat children – persuaded the government to accept their deletion (although it was emphasised that this would make 'no practical difference, because only "moderate and reasonable" punishment is lawful').[1] As the Bill passed through the House of Lords, Lord Herschell reassured peers that 'Your lordships will see that the Bill carefully reserves intact the power which rests in a parent or guardian to administer punishment to a child. In that respect the law is not interfered with by this Bill.'[2]

It appears that that was the last comment on this statutory endorsement of parents' rights to use physical punishment until a debate in the House of Lords on the Children Bill just 100 years later, in January 1989 (see page 106). The provision was re-enacted unchanged and without debate in the Prevention of Cruelty to Children Act 1894 (section 24), the Prevention of Cruelty to Children Act 1904 (section 28) and the Children and Young Persons Act 1933, which consolidated much earlier legislation. In Scotland and Northern Ireland, similar provisions with identical wording are included in the Children and Young Persons (Scotland) Act 1937 (section 12(7)), and the Children and Young Persons (Northern Ireland) Act 1950 (section 20(6)).

The 'right' reflected in the provision is the traditional common law freedom of parents and others caring for children to use 'moderate and reasonable' corporal punishment, set out in a series of early commentaries and cases mostly from the last century. In terms of technical legal language, the use of the word 'right' is mistaken. The words 'freedom' or 'privilege' are legally neutral. They imply the absence of a legal duty, and indicate that a parent does nothing wrong in physically chastising a child 'moderately and reasonably'. It is the common law which protects parents and others from civil proceedings and from risk of prosecution for criminal assault under the Offences Against the Person Act 1861 – unless the punishment goes beyond the courts' current interpretation of 'moderate and reasonable'. Halsbury's *Laws of England* provides this summary in its section on offences against the person, under 'Lawful correction': 'An act is not an assault if it is done in the course of the lawful correction of a child by its parent or of a pupil by its teacher, provided that the correction is reasonable and moderate considering the age and health of the child and administered with a proper instrument, and in the case of a female in a decent manner.'[3] A footnote indicates that 'the formerly recognised right to chastise servants, apprentices, mutinous seamen, etc. may be assumed to have fallen into desuetude'. Halsbury does not mention wife-beating, but other commentaries indicate that it, too, was at one time defended by the law. Bromley's *Family Law* quotes a 1736 authority stating that a husband might beat his wife 'but not in violent or cruel manner'; the commentary continues: '. . . whether he (the husband) ever had a legal right to administer corporal punishment is open to some doubt; Hale denied that he had, although Blackstone maintained that, whilst the practice had become obsolete in polite society, "the lower rank of people who were always fond of the old common law, still claim and exert their ancient privilege" '.[4]

In a case concerning the kidnapping of a wife in 1891, Lord Halsbury commented: '. . . such quaint and absurd dicta as are to be found in the books as to the right of a husband over his wife in respect of personal chastisement are not, I think, now capable of being cited as authorities in a court of justice in this or any civilized country'. He quoted with approval Hale's commentary in *Pleas of the Crown* in 1674 which suggested that husbands could admonish and confine but not beat their wives. Lord Halsbury was 'glad that some one even at that early period thought it inconsistent with the rights of free human creatures that such a power of personal chastisement of the wife should exist'.[5]

But such early feelings about the basic human rights of 'free human creatures' did not extend in the eyes of the law to children, and still do not.

Thus the same commentary quoted with approval by Lord Halsbury discussed 'a schoolmaster in reasonable manner beating his scholar, or father his son, or master his servant'. If 'by struggling the child or scholar or servant dies, this is only *per infortunium*'. And further on: 'If done with a cudgel or other thing not likely to kill, it will be manslaughter: if with a dangerous weapon likely to kill . . . or maim . . . murder . . . Yet though the correction exceeds the bounds of moderation, the court will pay a tender regard to the nature of the provocation.'[6]

Most of the relevant cases concern school beating rather than parental punishment. The leading case is *R.* v. *Hopley* [1860]. This was brought against a schoolmaster when a 13-year-old boy died as a result of being taken from his bed at night and beaten with a thick stick and a skipping rope for two and a half hours. The judge, Chief Justice Cockburn, held that the teacher was liable to a charge of manslaughter, and he was convicted. The judgment placed some limits on the concept of reasonable punishment:

> If it be administered for the gratification of passion or of rage, or if it be immoderate or excessive in its nature or degree, or if it be protracted beyond the child's powers of endurance, or with an instrument unfitted for the purpose and calculated to produce danger to life or limb; in all such cases the punishment is excessive, the violence is unlawful, and if evil consequences to life and limb ensue, then the person inflicting it is answerable to the law, and if death ensues, it will be manslaughter.

The Chief Justice emphasised: 'By the law of England, a parent . . . may for the purpose of correcting what is evil in the child, inflict moderate and reasonable corporal punishment, always, however, with this condition, that it is moderate and reasonable.'[7] In another case in 1869, *R.* v. *Griffin*, a father had beaten his daughter aged 2½ with a leather belt, causing her death. The defence submitted that no crime had been committed, the father having a perfect right to correct the child. But the judge held that the child must be capable of appreciating the punishment: 'The law as to correction has reference only to a child capable of appreciating correction, and not to an infant two and a half years old. Although a slight slap may be lawfully given to an infant by her mother, more violent treatment of an infant so young by her father would not be justifiable . . .'[8]

It is left to the judge or jury to decide what is meant by 'moderate and reasonable' in any particular case. In 1938, in a case concerning a child who had been struck on the head by his schoolmistress with the palm of the hand, rupturing his ear-drum and rendering him partly deaf in one ear, the judge commented: 'The blow struck was moderate in the sense that it was not a very violent blow, but as a punishment it was not moderate punishment because I do not think that the proper way of punishing a child is to strike it on the head or the ear.'[9] But there are no clear limits on where a child can be hit or with what. Thus, recently, magistrates dismissed a case against a father of causing actual bodily harm to his son who had been beaten by a belt causing bruising to the face; this was held to be acceptable chastisement.[10] In October 1985, a Staffordshire teacher, who burst a boy's eardrum by slapping him around the face, was acquitted of assault causing actual bodily harm. And, a week earlier, the deputy head of a school in Cornwall received an absolute discharge for hitting a 15-year-old girl with a walking stick, causing bruising.[11] (See also police and medical views of 'reasonable chastisement' in a tragic child abuse case in 1978, page 25.)

## Parents' Powers Today

The law has understandably avoided any attempt at a clear definition of parents' rights or powers in relation to their children. The Children Act 1975 simply states that parental rights and duties 'are all the rights and duties which by law the mother and father have in relation to a legitimate child and his property'. And the Children Bill, currently (1989) being debated in Parliament and containing wide-ranging reforms of children's law, introduces a new concept of 'parental responsibility' with a similarly circular definition: '. . . all the rights, duties, powers, responsibilities and authority which by law a parent of a child has in relation to the child and his property'.

The most significant recent judgment on the relationship between parents' rights and children's rights is that of the House of Lords in the Gillick case. Mrs Victoria Gillick was challenging the legality of a Department of Health and Social Security circular which permitted doctors to give contraceptive advice and treatment to under 16-year-olds without the knowledge or consent of their parents. In the High Court her case was rejected, but Court of Appeal judges backed her and declared that the DHSS's advice was contrary to law. Finally, in October 1985 the highest court in the land, the House of Lords, reversed the Appeal Court decision by a majority of three to two. The judgment clearly dismisses the idea that parents have absolute authority over their children until they reach 18, the age of majority:

Having regard to the reality that a child becomes increasingly independent as it grew older and that parental authority dwindled correspondingly, the law did not recognise any rule of absolute parental authority until a fixed age. Instead, parental rights were recognised by the law only as long as they were needed for the protection of the child and such rights yielded to the child's right to make his own decisions when he reached a sufficient understanding and intelligence to be capable of making up his own mind.[12]

Mrs Gillick had lost and, in doing so, she had not merely defeated her own narrow purpose, but had provoked a radical enhancement of the rights of the child.

So to what extent does the Gillick reassessment reduce the 'right' of parents to punish their children physically? Two legal commentators gave their preliminary views in articles in the Children's Legal Centre magazine *Childright* in 1986. Stephen Sedley, QC, suggested that 'a parent still has the power to control a child by the use of physical violence or restraint wherever it is "reasonable" to do so'. But he believed the major premise of the judgment, which jettisoned the concept of authority as the source of parental rights and replaced it with the primacy of the child's welfare, did sustain the following propositions:

(1)     a parent has no right to strike or confine a child at will;
(2)     a child has a right to well-being which determines the extent of the parent's power of punishment or restraint;
(3)     the reasonableness of punishment or restraint is therefore determined not by seeing how far the parental urge has to be controlled for the child's welfare, but by deciding how far it is reasonable for the parent to go in promoting the child's welfare.

And the Law Lords' view that parental powers decline as children's capacity increases implied other propositions:

(1)     there comes a point in a normal child's development where the parent's power extends only to giving advice for the child to take or leave;
(2)     once the parental power has shrunk to this little measure, it excludes control;
(3)     the shift from control to advice is not a single turning point but a continuing process which differs from child to child and is not determined by age alone except at the extremes.[13]

John Eekelaar, a law lecturer at Oxford University and expert in family law, believes that the judgment can be interpreted as rendering physical punishment and restraint unlawful early in a child's life: once a child acquires sufficient capacity (both intellectual and emotional) in relation to a particular matter, any parental rights on that matter expire, so that even if restraint of the child would be reasonable in promoting the child's interests, such restraint would be unlawful if exercised against the child's will: 'A child, even a very young child, understands what it means to be smacked, or locked in a room, and does not consent.' Eekelaar concedes that some will argue that children cannot be expected to understand the full implications of, and rationale for, punishment. But he concludes that 'from the technical legal point of view assaulting and locking up children become unlawful early in a child's life'.[14]

Both John Eekelaar and Stephen Sedley make it clear that enforcing such a new interpretation of the law is not going to be easy. The principles which Stephen Sedley believes are inherent in the Law Lords' judgment cannot, he writes, 'directly overcome the reluctance of most courts in this country to protect children from adult assault – or as the courts tend to put it, their support for parental or custodial forms of discipline'.

But he does believe that a court can no longer simply ask itself whether the parties are in the relationship of parent and child and, if so, whether the force used was immoderate.

It must make a more realistic and sensitive appraisal of the child's understanding and capacity for making his or her own decisions (which includes the capacity for making mistaken decisions and learning by the mistakes). It must next ask whether the child was at or ... beyond the stage where control or physical "correction" was an appropriate way of promoting his or her welfare. If and only if the child's development is found not to have progressed beyond that stage can the assault begin to be justified.

There do not appear to have been any cases involving parental punishment since the Gillick judgment in which these various interpretations have been raised and argued.

From the child's point of view, the Gillick case has had a significant effect in upholding rights to self-determination within the narrower field of consent to medical treatment. These rights are now established and clearly stated in government circulars and official reports. The issue was raised, in particular, in the context of the Cleveland Inquiry into Child Abuse in 1987/88, in connection with examinations following allegations of sexual abuse. Official guidance issued at the same time as the inquiry's report in July 1988 confirms the independent rights of children with 'sufficient understanding' either to consent or to refuse consent to medical examinations.[15]

The Gillick case has undoubtedly encouraged the general direction of the current (1989) reform of children's law, which is towards recognising children's growing rights to self-determination as well as protection. The new Children Bill, for example, proposes that 16- and 17-year-olds, at least, should generally be able to make their own decisions about who they live with and who they have access to. As the Bill goes through Parliament, attempts are also being made to give some statutory recognition to the Gillick principle by insisting that, in relation to decisions about children in care, local authorities should be obliged not only to listen to children's views, but also to accept them when the children are judged to have 'sufficient understanding'.

It is hard to believe, however, that the judgment in itself will have any significant effect on the prevalence of, or attitudes to, the physical punishment of children in the UK, or even on the traditional unwillingness of courts to interfere with parents' rights to punish their children. As Michael Freeman, Professor of English Law at University College, London, wrote in *Childright* in October 1988, it is the judges who have created the doctrine that an assault is not an assault when it is physical punishment, and 'it is probably too late for them to remove it'.[16]

## Removing the Right to Hit Children

If physical punishment of children by parents and other carers is to be regarded in future as no different from any other kind of violence against people, then it would be logical for the criminal law on assault to apply to it. Given the established common law 'right' of parents to hit their children, a specific statutory statement will be needed to abolish this 'right'.

Other countries which have adopted principles prohibiting physical punishment have done so within their family law (see page 67). While no penalties are directly attached to these prohibitions, they do indicate quite explicitly that the fact that an assault forms part of the punishment of a child by the parent is no defence in a criminal prosecution. In the Scandinavian countries, this was not intended to lead, and has not in practice led, to a rush of children reporting their parents to the police. Nor has it led to more state intervention in family life, or to more children being taken into care (see page 86). There is no reason to think that similar changes in the UK would have these unintended and undesirable results either. The Children Bill, currently (1989) in Parliament, only permits children to be taken into care against their parents' wishes under very strict conditions. These are that the child has suffered, or is likely to suffer, significant harm and that this harm is attributable to the parents' standard of care being below that which it would be reasonable to expect from the parent of a similar child (or the child is beyond parental control).

'Harm' is defined as ill-treatment or impairment of health and development. The court additionally has to be satisfied that making a care order is better for the child than no order or another sort of order. Moreover, in every case, the court must give paramount consideration to the child's welfare, having regard to a list of factors including the child's own wishes. Local authorities are placed under a parallel duty to protect the welfare of children in need and 'so far as is consistent with that duty, to promote the upbringing of such children by their families'. They must therefore take steps to diminish the need to bring care proceedings. Thus even if physical punishment becomes unlawful it would not lead, by itself, to a care order.[17]

Prohibiting parental physical punishment in the UK would involve a statutory provision which explicitly removed parents' and other carers' common law freedom to use even 'moderate and reasonable' punishment. The criminal law on petty assaults would then apply equally to the physical punishment of children. An alternative reform, stopping short of 'criminalising' physical punishment, would follow the course adopted when school corporal punishment was abolished in the Education (No.2) Act 1986. Parliament expressly avoided making teachers who hit children liable to criminal prosecution, but they are liable to civil action. The legislation removes their common law defence of 'reasonable punishment' in any civil actions, but leaves it intact when it comes to criminal prosecution. In schools the new legislation has clearly had the desired effect; everyone knows that corporal punishment is illegal, and the definition of corporal punishment includes smacking, slapping and anything else which would constitute an assault. The 'Model Bill' (see Appendix 3, page 144) provides legislation to remove parents' and other carers' defence of moderate and reasonable chastisement. If sub-section 1(4) (printed in italics) is included, physical punishment does not become a criminal offence. At the same time, the explicit endorsement of physical punishment in the Children and Young Persons Act 1933 (see page 97) would need to be repealed, as would the equivalent provisions in the similar laws in Scotland and Northern Ireland.

There are, of course, vast differences between schools, which are in the public domain and where instances of corporal punishment are now most unlikely to go unnoticed and unreported, and private homes. But the primary purpose of legislating against parental punishment is not to make legal action possible, but to indicate clearly that such punishment is not acceptable, to change attitudes and ultimately to eliminate the practice.

The first attempts to challenge the legality of parental physical punishment in the UK in Parliament were made in January 1989, while the Children Bill was at its committee stage in the House of Lords. An amendment was tabled to repeal section 1(7) of the Children and Young Persons Act 1933. The all-party group of peers sponsoring the amendment saw the repeal of section 1(7) as a first step – a way of indicating that physical punishment no longer has explicit support in children's legislation, and as a basis for further public debate and education. Whether the repeal by itself would have much effect on the courts' interpretation of parents' powers to hit children is doubtful. Section 1(7), preserving parents' and others' rights to punish children, appears explicitly to de-criminalise even those forms of physical punishment 'likely to cause unnecessary suffering or injury to health'. Under common law, such punishment only becomes criminal when the harm it does leads to it being regarded as not 'moderate and reasonable'. So the repeal of section 1(7) could at least lead to punishment 'likely to cause unnecessary suffering or injury to health' being seen as cruelty and thus a criminal offence. On the other hand, given the courts' clear reluctance to interfere with parents' rights to punish, it is quite likely that they would continue to uphold the view expressed by Halsbury's *Laws* that an assault is not an assault if it is 'moderate and reasonable' parental punishment.

The law prohibiting cruelty to animals (currently the Protection of Animals Act 1911) makes it an offence for anyone to 'cruelly beat, kick, ill treat . . . torture, infuriate or terrify any animal . . . or by wantonly or unreasonably doing or omitting any act . . . cause any unnecessary suffering'. Thus the repeal of section 1(7) of the 1933 Act could, at least, help to extend to children the protection afforded animals against 'unnecessary suffering'.

In the first of three short debates in the House of Lords on the amendment, during committee stage on 23 January 1989, the Lord Chancellor suggested that it would cause 'a serious ambiguity where none exists at the moment', and that it would create 'complete obscurity'.[18] The Children's Legal Centre sought a legal opinion on the effect of the repeal and the Lord Chancellor's view from Stephen Sedley, QC, who concluded: 'In my respectful opinion . . . the repeal of section 1(7) would be neither otiose nor a source of doubt. It would unify the law of cruelty so as to make it clear that parents have no special right to be cruel to their children in breach of section 1(1), but only the well-established right, for which section 1(7) is not required, to punish with restraint and moderation.'[19]

At report stage in the House of Lords in February, Lord Henderson moved the same amendment again, quoting Stephen Sedley's opinion and adding: 'Surely it is uncontroversial, given our heightened awareness and concern about child abuse, that parents must be given a clear message that punishment amounting to cruelty – that is, punishment which is "likely to cause unnecessary suffering or injury" – is abuse and should be treated as abuse.' Supporting the amendment, Baroness David said: 'It is high time that we took the first step towards ending the acceptability of physical punishment in our society. That is the serious purpose of the amendment.' The Lord Chancellor declined to give a government view of parents' rights to use physical punishment, but said that he did not favour the amendment; if the law was to be altered, 'then it should be altered in a principled way and not by this type of amendment'.[20]

When the same amendment was again debated during the Children Bill's Third Reading, on 16 March 1989, Lord Henderson pressed the Lord Chancellor to make a statement on government policy. The Lord Chancellor replied: 'My Lords, I have no statement to make, apart from stating the existing law, I have no proposals to put forward on behalf of the government for any change in the law'. It remained the government's view that the amendment would 'create obscurity'. The amendment was not pressed to a vote.[21]

## Physical Punishment in Institutions

On 15 August 1987, the UK became the last country in Europe to provide schoolchildren in state-supported education with legal protection against corporal punishment. The history of the campaign to achieve this long-overdue reform is summarised in Chapter 5. This section summarises the current law applying to schools and to other institutions where children live or spend some time.

The Education (No.2) Act 1986 removes the defence which teachers had previously been able to produce in any action against them for using physical punishment: that under common law they were entitled to administer 'moderate and reasonable' punishment (see Appendix 4, page 146). Punishment that goes beyond the courts' interpretation of 'moderate and reasonable' has always rendered teachers liable to criminal prosecution, and that is unaltered. But while the Education Act now means that teachers who punish pupils using any physical force are liable to civil proceedings, section 47(4) specifically avoids making 'moderate and reasonable' punishment a criminal offence.

Corporal punishment is defined as anything done to punish a pupil which would constitute a battery – thus it includes smacking, slapping, hitting with implements, throwing missiles, shaking, pulling hair, etc. Acts done to avert an immediate danger of personal injury or damage to property are excluded, but the force used must be reasonable. The law covers all state schools, and also protects pupils attending independent schools who are receiving government grants, and any pupils at such schools whose fees are paid wholly or partly by central or local government. But pupils at independent schools whose parents are paying their fees in full remain unprotected.

Following Parliament's decision to abolish school corporal punishment, the DHSS indicated that it intended to ensure that such punishment was also prohibited in the various categories of children's homes. In a parliamentary written answer in March 1987 to a question from Conservative MP Robert Key (who had played a crucial role in the final stage of abolishing school beating, see page 122), junior health minister Edwina Currie said:

> Completion of the revised regulations governing the conduct of local authority community homes and of voluntary children's homes is planned for later this year. At the same time it is intended to introduce regulations governing the conduct of private children's homes. A provision will be included in all these regulations prohibiting the use of corporal punishment in each type of establishment.

Mrs Currie went on to indicate that physical punishment would also be banned in residential care homes (mostly homes for elderly people, but containing some children with disabilities).[22] While the promised regulations applying to local authority, voluntary and private children's homes have still not appeared (May 1989 – delayed, according to the Department of Health, by the Children Bill now before Parliament), new regulations applying to residential care homes came into effect on 1 August 1988, stating that homes must ensure 'that corporal punishment is not used as a sanction in relation to any child in the home'.[23]

Mrs Currie was also asked about children in day nurseries and other provision for the under-fives (pupils at state nursery schools run by education authorities are covered by the new protection in education law). She replied:

> There are no circumstances in which corporal punishment

would be appropriate for children attending local authority day nurseries or any premises registered under the Nurseries and Childminders Registration Act 1948 (private nurseries). This subject has not been covered in departmental guidance, but it is intended that future guidance on day care services for pre-school children will deal with the question of discipline.

Referring to youth treatment centres – there are currently two such centres run directly by the Department of Health, providing mostly locked accommodation for very disturbed children – Mrs Currie said that corporal punishment had never been permitted (no specific regulations apply to the centres): 'It would be incompatible with the care and treatment which this service provides for the country's most disturbed boys and girls.'[24]

The Children's Legal Centre believes that there should be primary legislation, similar to that in education law, protecting children from physical punishment in all the various institutions run by health authorities, social services departments and voluntary and private bodies. Writing to the Health Secretary, Kenneth Clarke, in August 1988, the legal centre said that while it welcomed the various proposed reforms, it would like to see comprehensive protection: 'We believe that hitting has no place in the upbringing of children and that the State, when assuming parental control of children, should set an example of good parenting.' It drew attention to one type of institution – private homes catering for children and young people categorised as mentally disturbed – for which it appeared no protection against corporal punishment was planned. These homes are governed by the Nursing Homes and Mental Nursing Homes Regulations (which also cover all private health establishments), but although the regulations were amended at the same time as the Residential Care Homes Regulations, no prohibition of corporal punishment was included. The health service has shown a particular resistance to any regulations which limit treatment, traditionally a matter for professional discretion. But it seems quite wrong that those working in hospitals and nursing homes should retain a right to use physical punishment on children in their care (implied by the Children and Young Persons Act 1933 – see page 97 above), while those in schools and children's homes do not. It has been suggested that the various ethical codes of the health professions would prevent them using physical punishment – but that is no argument against establishing a clear legal principle that such punishment is unacceptable.

Foster care lies somewhere between institutional care and family care in private homes: currently foster parents are as able as parents to use physical punishment with impunity. By 1983, however, a Children's Legal Centre survey revealed that at least 10 English local authority social services departments had forbidden foster parents to hit children in their care.[25] In parts of Canada[26] and in 26 American states,[27] physical punishment by foster parents is forbidden in law – as it is, of course, in the Scandinavian countries and Austria. When the Department of Health was consulting on revised regulations to govern foster care in 1988, the Children's Legal Centre commented:

> Surprisingly there is no mention of discipline at any point in the draft regulations or guidance. We understand that forthcoming regulations governing the other placements for children in care explicitly prohibit corporal punishment of children, as well as other forms of humiliating and degrading treatment. The Government should take the valuable opportunity offered here to ensure children in care have consistent protection from unconstructive forms of punishment ... We strongly urge you to prohibit the use of corporal punishment in foster-care in the regulations.[28]

An amendment to the Children Bill, seeking to prohibit foster parents from hitting children, was promoted by the legal centre when the Bill was in the House of Lords in January 1989. Although it had the unanimous support of child care organisations, including the National Foster Care Association, the amendment was defeated by a majority of 19 votes.[29]

It is clear that the UK has now (March 1989) got as far as deciding that children should not be hit in institutions by those teaching or looking after them (with the curious exception of pupils paid for by their parents in private schools). While the legal prohibitions are not yet comprehensive, and quite a lot of detailed tidying up needs to be done to ensure consistent legal protection for all children and young people, the principle seems to have been established at last. It may be that the arguments for extending this protection to foster children will still prevail during the course of the current Children Bill. If that is the case, it will leave parents and others – apart from foster parents – who have 'custody, charge or care' of a child, but do not work in institutional settings (that is, relatives, baby sitters, etc.) with a defence in law if they use 'moderate and reasonable' physical punishment against that child.

The state has, to a significant degree, withdrawn its seal of approval from hitting children. The inevitable next step is to acknowledge that in no setting can physical punishment be justified, and in every setting it can be harmful, and to legislate accordingly.

# CHAPTER 5

---

# THE LONG STRUGGLE TO END SCHOOL BEATING IN THE UK

*'Corporal punishment is regarded by many knowledgeable and responsible educationists as a valuable disciplinary instrument. We should not lightly deprive them of it.'*

(Chris Patten, junior education minister,
House of Commons, *Hansard*, 22 July 1986, col. 273)

The history of attempts to end school beating in the UK is included in this book because it illustrates the incredible tenacity with which teachers' leaders and local and national politicians, generally aided by the public and always by the judiciary, clung to a practice that had long been discredited as dangerous and anti-educational. It is a story which shows how deeply ingrained the institutionalised hitting of children had become in our society.

On 15 August 1987, the UK became the last European country to end school corporal punishment. In the House of Commons, abolitionists had won by a single vote. But, even now, pupils paid for by their parents at private schools can still be beaten – the ban only applies to state-supported education: state schools, private schools receiving state grants and pupils at private schools financially supported in part or wholly by the state (see page 107 and Appendix 4, page 146 for details of the law).

The earliest recorded attempt to persuade Parliament to end school beating was in 1669. A 'lively boy' presented a petition 'on behalf of the children of this nation', to protest against 'that intolerable grievance our youth lie under, in the accustomed severities of the school discipline of this nation'.[1] The chronology in Appendix 1 details significant events along the path towards the abolition of physical punishment in schools, other institutions and the home from this date over three centuries.

The story of how school abolition was finally achieved began in

1966, when a new recruit to teaching in a London school, Gene Adams, was concerned to see a senior master waging a 'personal war' against an 11-year-old boy, including weekly canings: 'The master commented in an end-of-term report on the boy's achievements in English that he was "feeble, vicious and obscene". The teacher went on to become head of another school, and has now retired amidst clouds of glory with an OBE. Heaven knows what happened to the boy. When I last saw him, his one ambition was to join a demolition firm and demolish the school.' Gene Adams was disturbed to find she had joined a profession 'which not only justified violence to its clients but even organised its unions partly to "give protection" against awkward parents'. Her discovery led her to discuss with trusted colleagues and people involved in the National Council for Civil Liberties what could be done to end physical punishment in schools. She was also influenced by the experience of Ivor Cook, a worker at Court Lees Approved School who, in 1967, revealed details of beatings there. These led to an inquiry, an immediate halving of the rate of the use of the cane in all approved schools, and to the end of his professional career.

In September 1968, Gene Adams and others launched the Society of Teachers Opposed to Physical Punishment (STOPP) at a public meeting in Caxton Hall, Westminster. Its first chairman was another teacher, John Holland, who was succeeded a few years later by Nick Peacey. Twenty years later, in February 1989, the STOPP membership decided to wind up the organisation, its aim almost achieved.

STOPP must be thanked for keeping the issue in the public eye over the last two decades, and for persuading many educational organisations and politicians of the case for abolition. Those who started the society, and worked for it as volunteers and paid staff, at times faced ridicule and abuse, even damage to their careers. Hopefully, one day the full and absorbing story of STOPP's 20-year war against school beating will be written.

Credit for the acronym which helped to establish STOPP in the media and the public conscience goes to Colin Rendell Brown, who had spent a year in advertising before going into teaching. As an organisation, it had some ups and downs, like all similar small pressure groups. There were crisis meetings in the mid-1970s when it looked as though it might disband, then a period of renewed energy with Croydon teachers, Colin Bagnall and Stephen Rogers, as honorary secretary and membership secretary respectively. In 1979 STOPP employed Tom Scott as its full-time education secretary and, later, Paul Temperton was appointed as its first part-time research co-ordinator.

But the society, whose membership never exceeded 1,000, was always tiny in relation to the size of the task and the number of its confessed enemies. Membership subscriptions and individual donations were an important part of STOPP's often precarious finances. The Joseph Rowntree Charitable Trust, prevented by law from supporting STOPP's campaigning work, was able to finance research and education which underpinned the campaign, and the trustees' initiative encouraged other smaller trusts and foundations to help too. Without such grants, it would not have been possible to employ full- and part-time workers.

## The Role of the European Commission and Court of Human Rights

In retrospect, undoubtedly the crucial event of the campaign against school beating was the decision of the European Court of Human Rights in February 1982 that the UK was in breach of the Human Rights Convention by not respecting parents' objections to corporal punishment.[2] This forced the government's hand and ultimately led to abolition. It was ironic, perhaps, that this decision should rest on parents' rather than children's rights, given that the whole problem of physical punishment derives from parents' traditional rights to hit their children, and the assumption that these rights are delegated to teachers and others *in loco parentis*. In 1976 two Scottish mothers, Mrs Grace Campbell and Mrs Jane Cosans, aided by a sympathetic and very energetic lawyer, Norman MacEwan (who sadly died in 1988), applied to the European Human Rights Commission in Strasbourg. They alleged that the UK was in breach of the European Human Rights Convention because corporal punishment, used in the schools attended by their sons, was contrary to article 3: 'No-one shall be subjected to torture or to inhuman or degrading treatment or punishment.' The government had also failed to respect their objections to this form of punishment which was in breach of article 2 of protocol 1 to the Convention: 'No person shall be denied the right to education. In the exercise of any functions which it assumes in relation to education and to teaching, the State shall respect the rights of parents to ensure such education and teaching in conformity with their own religious and philosophical convictions.'

Gordon Campbell, then aged 6, was attending a school which used corporal punishment, and his mother was refused a guarantee that he would not be subjected to it. (In the event, he was never hit.) Jeffrey Cosans, then aged 15, was told on 23 September 1976 to report to the assistant head of his school on the following day, according to the Commission's report, 'to receive corporal punishment for having tried to take a prohibited short cut through a cemetery on his way home from school. On his father's advice Jeffrey duly reported, but refused to accept the punishment. On that account he was immediately suspended from school until such time as he was willing to accept the punishment.' In January 1977, the Fife Regional Council, which was responsible for the school, said that the suspension could be lifted provided 'Jeffrey will obey the rules, regulations or disciplinary requirements of the school'. Mr and Mrs Cosans insisted that they must have a guarantee that corporal punishment would not be used. This was unacceptable to the council, so Jeffrey never returned to school. Mrs Cosans's application alleged, in addition, that his suspension had breached his 'right to education', guaranteed by article 2 of protocol 1.

As neither boy had in fact received corporal punishment, the European Commission rejected the allegation that their treatment breached Article 3, but they found that there had been a failure to respect the parents' philosophical convictions, guaranteed by article 2 of protocol 1. A majority concluded that it was not necessary to consider, in addition, whether Jeffrey Cosans's right to education had also been breached.[3]

Throughout this and the many other cases involving school beatings that have been taken to the commission by parents and children over the last 12 years, the UK government has spared no expense in defending corporal punishment at every stage. Some cases are still not settled in 1989. In Strasbourg, where the Council of Europe's Commission and Court of Human Rights are sited, the procedure for dealing with applications from individuals is lengthy. First, the commission considers whether there is a case to be answered (whether the application is 'admissible'). Then there is a period during which the facts are established in detail and the commission seeks to reach a 'friendly settlement' between the applicant(s) and the government of the country complained of. If this fails, a report goes to the Committee of Ministers of the Council of Europe, and within a period of three months the case can be referred to the Court of Human Rights by the state concerned or by the commission (not by the applicant). If the case does not go to the court, a final decision on any action to be taken is made by the Committee of Ministers.

The case of Campbell and Cosans was referred to the court by the commission in October 1980, and two years later, on 25 February 1982, the court issued its judgment. It confirmed the commission's view that no breach of article 3 had been established, but that article 2 of protocol 1 had been breached, because the parents' objections to corporal punishment had not been respected and Jeffrey Cosans had also been denied his right to education. Jeffrey Cosans was eventually awarded £3,000 'moral damages', and the government was ordered to pay the families' legal costs.

This judgment was the turning point: from then on the days of legalised school beating were numbered. A few days later, as part of the 'friendly settlement' in another case declared admissible by the Human Rights Commission, the government was forced to send a circular letter to all local education authorities stating that 'the use of corporal punishment may in certain circumstances amount to treatment contrary to Article 3'. That case (*Mrs X v. UK*) involved a 14-year-old girl who had been caned by her headmistress: 'A doctor found that this caning had produced weals on the buttocks (one over a foot long) and hand. The child was in discomfort for several days and traces of the caning remained for a considerably longer period.'[4]

There has, as yet, been no final ruling from the European Court of Human Rights that school corporal punishment is 'degrading' in breach of article 3. The commission has, however, concluded in one case that article 3 was breached. At present (1989) still awaiting a final decision from the Committee of Ministers, the application in this case was made by a mother and her then 16-year-old daughter (*Mrs X and Miss X v. UK*). The young woman was seen by the male head smoking with two other girls in the street outside her school. She and one other girl were caned by the headmaster; the punishment was administered on the left hand in the presence of the deputy head – another man. The caning caused two large bruises on her palm, which were still visible when she was examined by a doctor eight days later. She complained to the police, but after interviewing the head they decided that the nature of the injury did not justify prosecution. Complaints to the education authority were also rejected, and the mother failed to get an assurance that corporal punishment would not be used on her other daughter at the same school. The mother then brought a civil action, but this was dismissed by the court on the ground that the punishment was not 'improper, inappropriate or disproportionate'. In its report, the commission, concluding that there had been a breach of article 3, said it had had 'special regard to the distinctive circumstances surrounding the use of corporal punishment' in the case:

It attaches particular importance to the fact that the punishment consisted of a physical injury inflicted by a man, in the presence of another man, on a 16-year-old girl ... In addition the injury ... cannot be said to have been of a merely trivial nature. Nor can it be excluded that the punishment also had adverse psychological effects.

Consequently, considering these circumstances as a whole, the Commission finds that the corporal punishment inflicted ... caused her humiliation and attained a sufficient level of seriousness to be regarded as degrading within the meaning of Article 3.[5]

More than 20 other successful applications have been made by families with the support of STOPP (and some others, independent of STOPP). In financial terms, the cost to the government has been large – probably over £4 million. As part of the settlements, families have received between £3,000 and £4,750 each as *ex gratia* payments. A number of cases involving corporal punishment at private (independent) schools are still being considered by the commission in Strasbourg. It is interesting to note that a STOPP survey in 1987 and 1988 of 501 independent secondary schools found that 42 (8 per cent) used corporal punishment, 299 (60 per cent) said that they did not use it, 2 refused to say and 158 did not reply.[6]

## The Sudden Conversion of the Teacher Unions

The first effect of the Campbell and Cosans judgment was to convince some of the teacher unions, which up to then had generally maintained a vigorous opposition to abolition, that they should change their beating policies before they were forced to. The 1982 Conference of the National Union of Teachers (NUT) overwhelmingly passed a resolution opposing the use of corporal punishment in all schools. The following year, the National Association of Head Teachers (NAHT), the Secondary Heads' Association, the Ulster Teachers' Union and the National Association of Welsh Teachers followed suit.

By the time of the parliamentary decision to abolish in 1986, the major unions had completed their about-turn. Thus the NUT declared that the decision was 'a milestone', and the National Association of Head Teachers said: 'We regard the vote as a victory for common sense.' But, without any doubt, it was the teachers who had kept the 'milestone' out of sight and had defied common sense for decades. Teacher members of STOPP played a vital part in, first, persuading one or two local branches of the NUT to come out against beating, then getting resolutions tabled at annual conferences, at which STOPP held 'fringe' press conferences. One of its essential roles, particularly in later years, was to cut through the use of respectable and clinical terms like 'administering corporal punishment'. STOPP's press releases therefore used words such as 'beating', 'thrashing' or 'lashes of the cane' to get across the degree of pain and humiliation involved.

The only significant measure of success that STOPP had before Parliament voted for abolition was the number of local education authorities implementing abolitionist policies in their schools. In 1930 a sub-area of one education authority banned corporal punishment after a teacher had injured a pupil, but it was reintroduced following teacher, police and parental protests 18 months later. Cardiff attempted to ban the cane in its primary schools for an experimental period in 1968, but opposition from local branches of the NUT and NAHT led to its reintroduction within two months. In January 1973, the Inner London Education Authority banned corporal punishment in its primary schools; Haringey became the first authority to ban it in all its schools in 1979. Local education authorities could not, however, impose such a ban on voluntary-aided (mainly church) schools in their area.[7] Therefore STOPP's role in persuading the established churches to take a stance against corporal punishment was crucial. In 1982 the Church of England General Synod Board of Education called on all its Anglican schools to 'phase out and ultimately abolish the practice'. The Catholic Education Council advised its schools similarly in 1983. Another barometer of progress was the slow conversion of a whole range of professional organisations – of doctors, psychologists, psychiatrists, social workers, etc. – to the abolitionist cause. A working party of the British Psychological Society, convened by Bob Green, a STOPP committee member and professor of psychology, and including STOPP sponsor Penelope Leach, produced an influential report in 1980.[8] STOPP had a number of distinguished sponsors, including philosopher Sir Alfred Ayer, Lord Soper, Bishop Trevor Huddleston and the late Baroness Wootton of Abinger. Lady Plowden, whose report on primary schools had advocated abolition in 1967, later became the society's patron.

STOPP also had constantly to challenge the suggestion that beating was dying out of its own accord. (It had to be remembered that as far back as 1937, a joint memorandum from the NUT and the Association of Education Committees had stated: 'Corporal punishment is rapidly disappearing from public elementary schools.') Thus, in 1981 STOPP published *A Quarter of a Million Beatings*,[9] the estimated annual total of recorded beatings in England alone. And in 1983 the society published *Once Every Nineteen Seconds*, reflecting its 'conservative estimate' of the frequency of school beatings in England and Wales, based on punishment book statistics published by 27 local education authorities.[10]

Use of these statistics was another key strategy in the campaign. Every school was obliged to keep a book recording all instances of punishment (but it was clear from STOPP informants that a great deal of school beating was never in fact recorded). In the earlier days of the campaign, some teachers risked dismissal to 'leak' statistics to STOPP. For example, a Liverpool teacher, Alan Corkish, who gave STOPP information indicating that during 1979/80, 1,985 slipperings were inflicted on pupils during four terms at Litherlands High School, Sefton, was subsequently sacked. Later, abolitionist councillors in many areas insisted on the publication of such statistics, thereby speeding the end of school beating in many local education authorities.

Alan Corkish was just one of several martyrs in STOPP's cause, who included heads sacked for refusing to use the cane, the most illustrious probably being Michael Duane whose story was told in Leila Berg's book *Risinghill: Death of a Comprehensive*.[11] Parents were pilloried and even lost their children to state care because they would not allow them to be beaten in school. But, as an article in *The Times Educational Supplement* put it in 1987, 'the real martyrs in their millions are those children and young people who have been forced to endure the sordid reality and the pain, whose educational experience has been scarred by often ritualized institutional violence on a massive scale'.[12]

STOPP had to find, and constantly keep in the public eye, research demonstrating the ineffectiveness of corporal punishment (repetition of the same names in punishment books remains the most graphic illustration of this) and its real and potential dangers. One sad, sordid and very common phenomenon which had to be exposed was that of the many people who, as a result of school and/or home beatings, derived sexual pleasure from giving or receiving corporal punishment. Individuals who had suffered wrote to STOPP. The society drew attention to the vast range of specialist pornography and interviewed specialist members of the English Collective of Prostitutes. Much of the pornography depicted typical school discipline scenes. STOPP even found that its own publications and press releases, and information about European cases, had been incorporated into magazines such as *Janus, Kane, Martinet, Spanking and Corporal Punishment Review*, and so on.

Its cause was not helped by one member who was found to have been writing frequently to newspapers supporting corporal punishment – using a woman's alias and a false address. The letters often related the 'woman's' beating experiences in salacious detail, and 'she' also contributed to *Kane*.

STOPP also investigated the cane manufacturers, including Eric Huntingdon whose company provided canes for school and home use until 1986. Then the *Daily Telegraph* reported: 'The Bognor Cane Company, formerly Britain's major punishment cane suppliers, under threat of extinction following the Commons' decision last week to abolish corporal punishment, has been bought by Mr Dai Llewellyn, socialite, club proprietor and Old Etonian.' The *Telegraph* also reported that 'The purchase is bad news for horses, as Mr Llewellyn is to concentrate on producing equestrian canes'.[13] Mr Huntingdon indicated that he had moved into campaigning 'against food additives and their effect on the permissive society'. According to the *Telegraph*, Mr Huntingdon once launched a pressure group of his own known as SLAPP (Sensible, Loving and Practical Parents) 'to promote the notion of firm discipline in the home'. He also published, at least until 1986, a magazine called *Family View*, often filled with descriptions of beating methods adopted by correspondents describing themselves as parents.

The royal family did not escape STOPP's attention. In 1984, for instance, it objected to Prince Andrew, now Duke of York, attending a reunion of the squadron with which he served in the South Atlantic, at a restaurant club called School Dinners. For here, according to the *Daily Mail*, 'the waitresses wear black stockings, short skirts – to show their garters and suspenders – school blouses and ties, a "headmistress" canes "naughty" diners who refuse to eat their greens or get cheeky with the girls'.[14] STOPP also challenged Prince Charles's and Prince Edward's sympathetic remarks about corporal punishment at their school, Gordonstoun. Courteous replies from private secretaries indicated that their royal highnesses had 'taken note' of STOPP's comments.

## The Path to Parliamentary Abolition

Over the years, STOPP had received frequent letters from officials and ministers at the Department of Education and Science, in response to pleas for action and complaints about excessive beating at individual schools. (Another vital role for STOPP was hounding the minority of true sadists who found an easy outlet for their perversion in the education system.) As late as November 1981, a few months before the European Court judgment, DES officials were still reiterating that 'the position with regards to the use of corporal punishment in England and Wales is well known to you and the Government has no plans to change the law in this respect'.[15] After the judgment, the government still dragged its feet as long as possible. Finally, in January 1985, the Education (Corporal Punishment) Bill was presented to the House of Commons. The Secretary of State for Education, Sir Keith Joseph (now Lord Joseph), admitted that had he been given a choice, 'this is not the subject on which we would have been legislating'.[16] The Bill, and incredibly complex regulations to be issued under it, would have enabled parents to exempt their children from corporal punishment in state schools, as a minimalist response to the European Court judgment. The Bill was quickly labelled 'dotty', 'totally unsatisfactory', 'lacking morality', or 'a system of apartheid' by a vast range of critics. All the teacher unions accepted that abolition would be preferable to the implementation of an unjust 'opt-out' scheme.[17]

STOPP and the Children's Legal Centre co-ordinated parliamentary opposition. On 4 July 1985, following extensive lobbying, the House of Lords voted by 108 votes to 104 to turn the Education (Corporal Punishment) Bill into an abolitionist measure. Baroness David, then Labour's spokeswoman on education in the Lords, led the opposition. She was supported by three Conservatives (including Baroness Elliott of Harwood, a long-standing supporter of abolition, who had been a member of the Advisory Council which in 1960 argued strongly against the reintroduction of judicial corporal punishment), 11 Social Democrats, 12 Liberal, 14 cross-benchers and 68 Labour peers. Baroness Wootton of Abinger, whose own Bill to abolish school beating had been defeated in the Lords in 1973, said in the debate: 'Perhaps I might refer once again to my friends, the Russian children, who, when our English party arrived, greeted us all with a warm handshake and the moving words, 'So you come from Britain, where they beat the children?'' [18] A few weeks after the vote, the government indicated that it was not proceeding with the Bill.

In 1986 the Secretary of State for Education, Kenneth Baker, introduced a new Education Bill, which started its passage in the House of Lords. It was silent on the issue of corporal punishment, but during committee stage in the Lords on 17 April, peers voted by a majority of 2 (94 to 92) to add an abolitionist amendment initiated by STOPP and the Children's Legal Centre.[19] When the Bill got to the Commons, Kenneth Baker indicated that the government would allow a free vote on whether to retain corporal punishment or not. If (as he personally hoped) corporal punishment was to be retained, school governing bodies, heads and parents would decide whether to use it and would also have to find 'suitable arrangements' to ensure that the 'philosophical convictions' of parents were respected. The Children's Legal Centre sought a legal opinion from two eminent practitioners in European human rights law – Anthony Lester, QC, and David Pannick – who argued that if Mr Baker's plans were followed, the UK would remain in breach of the European Human Rights Convention.[20]

STOPP's two paid workers, Martin Rosenbaum and Julie Macfarlane, helped by the Children's Legal Centre, then embarked on an intensive and carefully targeted lobbying exercise of MPs of all parties. Certain Conservative MPs, in particular STOPP sponsor Robert Key, played important roles. STOPP was also helped by a photograph which appeared in an early edition of the *Evening Standard* on the day of the vote, 22 July: it showed appalling bruising on the buttocks of a 13-year-old boy five days after he had been caned. Barry Tavner had been beaten by the head of Friern Barnet Grammar School, a north London private school, for not doing well enough in an exam, and his mother had contacted the STOPP office five days before the debate. (Later, a Crown Court judge directed a jury to acquit the headteacher, John Pearman. The judge, Christopher Hordern, QC, also said to the prosecuting counsel: 'Can you really say with a straight face that five strokes of the cane is unreasonable? If one has the misfortune to be caned, one expects to be hit rather hard. That's the point of it . . . It would be a slightly odd caning if considerable force were not used.')[21] Just before the debate, STOPP circulated copies of the *Standard* story and photograph to dozens of those MPs thought to be 'waverers'. This was a particularly important example of the frequent use which STOPP made of individual cases to illustrate to the public the reality of school beating from the perspective of the children receiving it. Parents and children frequently phoned or wrote to the STOPP office for advice and help. There was no question of revealing their names or their experiences without their express permission, but many became strong long-term supporters of the society.

The division in the House of Commons – and victory by 231 votes to 230 – came at the end of a three-and-a-half-hour debate. Thirty-seven Conservatives, including eight ministers, joined the opposition parties in voting for abolition – against the advice of Kenneth Baker. His junior minister, Chris Patten, spoke strongly for retention: 'Corporal punishment is regarded by many knowledgeable and responsible educationists as a valuable disciplinary instrument. We should not lightly deprive them of it.'[22] The government then indicated that abolition would take effect throughout England, Wales, Scotland and Northern Ireland on 15 August 1987.[23]

STOPP remained in existence for a further year and a half, to monitor the implementation of abolition, to continue to press for its extension to fully cover the independent sector, and to handle the remaining casework, including applications to the European Human Rights Commission. The final annual general meeting, late in 1988, was told that the Children's Legal Centre would carry on these functions, and passed a resolution to disband. The membership was balloted and agreed to this; as its final act, STOPP's committee decided to pass on the residue of its funds to the new organisation EPOCH – End Physical Punishment of Children (see page 175) now campaigning to end physical punishment in the home.

# CHAPTER 6

# WHAT CAN BE DONE NOW: NEXT STEPS IN THE UK

*'Changing child-rearing practices might be the single most important action we can take as a society on behalf of today's children, and on behalf of tomorrow's parents. If we can discourage the use of force and encourage the use of open and honest physical affection within the family, this might prove to be a formidable goal and a worthwhile cause.'*

(Joan Senzek Solheim, educational co-ordinator,
C. Henry Kempe National Center for the Prevention and Treatment of Child
Abuse and Neglect)

The introduction indicated that 1989 has already seen a challenge in the UK Parliament to parents' rights to hit children. It was probably the first challenge, and certainly the first in recent times. The Children Bill is still in Parliament (May 1989), but it seems unlikely that there will be sudden agreement to prohibit parental punishment.

The issue must be kept in the public eye; the continuing unprecedented level of concern over child abuse should see to that. As mentioned at the end of the last chapter, 1989 also sees the formation of a new organisation, EPOCH. This will provide one focus for the various strategies – information, education, research and legal reforms – needed to persuade parents and other carers not to hit children. An early task for EPOCH will be to try and persuade a variety of organisations of parents and professionals to support its aims.

The campaign to end school corporal punishment described in the preceding chapter had a single goal – legislation. Because teachers were hitting children in the fairly public arena of the education system, it was safe to assume that once the law prohibited school corporal punishment, few teachers were going to persist and thus risk their reputation and their jobs, let alone being dragged through the courts. Thus, even before the 1986 parliamentary vote to abolish beating in schools, campaigners were able to measure their success by the gradually increasing numbers of individual schools and – more significantly – local education authorities which resolved to ban beating.

## Legal Changes and Public Education

It will not be so easy to measure the success of the campaign to end physical punishment in the home, as only parents and children will know the true situation. The aims of the campaign are obviously directly linked to those of the long campaign in the education system, and are fundamentally about reducing the level and acceptability of violence in society, and improving the status of children. But it is quite clear that changing the law alone will not be enough. Previous chapters should have convinced readers that we are dealing with a deeply entrenched habit, something still viewed by a large majority as at least a right, and, in many cases, a duty. The strong reactions encountered by the Ritchies in New Zealand when they raised the issue of the abolition of physical punishment suggested to them that they had 'touched an exposed nerve in the national culture'.[1] Research has indicated that attitudes to the use of physical punishment are linked closely to whether or not respondents experienced it themselves (see page 82). The high rates of its prevalence among the current generation of UK parents implies that a great deal of attitude-changing must go on.

Law reform to prohibit physical punishment is certainly necessary: how else can we possibly avoid the current confusion over 'acceptable' levels of violence to children? But it is also vital that the purpose of legal changes should be promoted as clearly as it has been in the four Scandinavian countries that have prohibited hitting children. Recent media coverage of the issue in England has shown how some influential commentators are anxious to misinterpret the motivation for changing the law, and its likely effects. To spell it out again, the purpose is neither to punish parents, nor to increase the levels of state 'snooping' and intervention in families. The purpose is educational: to change attitudes by ensuring that there is a clear message that our society no longer tolerates the hitting of children. If we look at what has happened in Scandinavia, there is no reason whatsoever to believe that the legal changes outlined in Chapter 4 would lead to a rush of children reporting their parents to the police and dragging them into court, nor that they would lead to more social work intervention and to children being taken unwillingly into care.

Moreover, it must not be forgotten that we have not quite finished the job of ending the legalised hitting of children in institutions in the UK. The anomaly which continues to allow some pupils in independent schools to be beaten must be removed, and protection of children from physical punishment in other institutions and child care settings must be comprehensive. Chapter 5 summarised the long struggle to end school beating; surely extending the protection of children against physical punishment to their homes and other settings should now be a relatively short step.

Alongside efforts to convince Parliament to remove the legal seal of approval from physical punishment, there must be public education. The experience of Scandinavia shows how dramatically attitudes can be changed by intensive public campaigns. It also underlines the particular importance of targetting this education on children, as well as on all parents and the general public (hence the imaginative use in Sweden of messages on milk cartons, and of the school curriculum). There is already a substantial amount of written and other advice to parents on approaches to discipline which do not involve physical punishment (see Appendix 2). Unfortunately, there is also quite a lot of published material which positively encourages physical punishment. In the United States, a survey of 31 contemporary child-rearing manuals found that '29 per cent encourage the use of physical punishment, 35 per cent discourage it and 35 per cent do not address the topic'.[2] An early task for EPOCH will be to survey existing material in the UK, and to challenge any which gives dangerous advice.

There is a need for more imaginative and direct educational approaches, to ensure that helpful and relevant material, in one form or another, comprehensively reaches parents and parents-to-be. In schools, these approaches must permeate parent and social education courses (National Curriculum guidelines for teachers should explicitly discourage physical punishment). Hopefully, both statutory and voluntary organisations can join in getting the message across. It is encouraging that the National Society for the Prevention of Cruelty to Children, in a new parental education booklet, *Putting Children First*, comes down firmly against smacking and other aggressive parenting techniques which

> . . . will not teach children how to use self-control. Once they get used to angry, loud voices and smacks, you will find it much harder to control them by showing disappointment or disapproval or by using other gentle methods of persuasion.

This negative approach can also lead to a vicious circle, with you shouting louder and smacking harder to achieve the same result.

You should also think about how it makes your child feel. We don't hit other adults when we don't like their behaviour, so surely we should treat our children with the same respect.[3]

A National Children's Home leaflet, *Tips for Young Parents*, agrees with this advice: 'It is easier not to hit your child the first time, after that it becomes more difficult to stop.'[4]

A national public education campaign against physical punishment by parents is just getting under way in the United States. A meeting in February 1989 of 40 experts, sponsored by the American Academy of Pediatrics and other bodies, concluded:

Numerous studies have overwhelmingly proved that hitting, spanking, slapping and other forms of physical punishment are harmful methods of changing children's behaviour. Alternative forms of discipline are more effective. The use of physical punishment is deeply ingrained in American society and will be difficult to eliminate. Nevertheless, convincing evidence of the detrimental effects of physical punishment on children indicates that the time for action is immediate and urgent.

The campaign, emphasising that 'children should have the same protections and rights as adults do to be free from assault', will include public service television and radio announcements.[5]

## Social Changes and Support for Carers

EPOCH will of course support those involved in pressing for social reforms which reflect a higher priority for children and adequate support for those who bear the burden of child-rearing; social reforms which combat gross inequalities, poverty, homelessness, unemployment, and discrimination on grounds of disability, race and sex. The absence of adequate support, the prevalence of grinding poverty and discrimination do not justify hitting children. While society tolerates and the law endorses this particular form of violence, other social ills lead to more hitting and more extreme abuse. But we cannot wait for an improved social context before extending to children our general veto on violence.

There are other vital ways of improving the status of children; in particular, by insisting that their own views should be heard and taken seriously whenever decisions are being made about their lives, in the home, in institutions and in the courts. The Children Bill currently (May 1989) in Parliament makes substantial progress in recognising children's rights. Education law now lags far behind the other major legal frameworks which affect children, in that it makes no provision whatsoever for taking their views into account, despite providing a service which consumes such a large part of childhood.

EPOCH will support and encourage anything which reduces the immediate stress of day-to-day parenting. National and local organisations have developed a variety of community strategies aiming to help end the isolation of parenthood – still usually the isolation of motherhood, but there are many parents they do not yet reach. Adrienne Rich writes:

> What woman, in the solitary confinement of a life at home enclosed with young children, or in the struggle to mother them while providing for them single-handedly, or in the conflict of weighing her own personhood against the dogma that says she is a mother, first, last and always – what woman has not dreamed of "going over the edge", of simply letting go, relinquishing what is termed her sanity, so that she can be taken care of for once, or can simply find a way to take care of herself?[6]

Much of a practical nature can and must be done to avoid child/parent conflicts in the home and elsewhere. John and Elizabeth Newson report that 'the most important single geographical area in which the child's activities were likely to be punished was the fireplace and hearth . . . Another source of trouble was the exploration of various domestic appliances, especially of electrical gadgets. Switches, wall plugs and trailing flexes were frequently mentioned, and, in particular, radio and television control knobs . . .' Sixteen per cent of punished offences of 1-year-olds involved the fireplace and its equipment, and about another 13 per cent were connected with household appliances or electrical fittings.[7] It is no surprise to find that the countries which have prohibited physical punishment are also in the forefront of moves to reduce child accidents in the home. 'Childproofing' homes along Swedish lines (see page 84) is an obvious concept to develop. In the UK, health visitors and pre-natal and child health clinics have a crucial advice and support role.

Outside the home, too, critical children's and parents' eyes need to look over all public amenities; so much more could be done at so little cost to make our society more child-centred, and more welcoming to people with children and babies. 'We Welcome Small Children' is a national campaign launched in 1985 and rapidly growing. It aims to improve facilities for carers with small children and to encourage public places, such as shops, restaurants, and so on, to welcome them. There are 74 local campaign groups around the UK. Public places which meet criteria set by the group are awarded a 'We Welcome Small Children' window sticker and certificate. A recent newsletter announces that the London Borough of Ealing has adopted the aims of the campaign; Boots the Chemist has introduced changing and feeding facilities for babies at 100 branches, and Tesco's has indicated that 26 of its supermarkets are to have them shortly. (When will supermarkets remove those provocative child-level displays of sweets from the check-out area?) A survey by local groups confirmed some good developments, but reported a general lack of changing/feeding areas, play space and access for buggies. Transport was reported as 'the area of a carer's life presenting the biggest problem. Many members said travelling was dangerous, difficult and exhausting with baby/toddler, pushchair, shopping etc.'[8]

The group, collaborating with the Women's Design Service and the London Borough of Camden, has also published a booklet, *Thinking of Small Children: Access, Provision and Play*, aimed particularly at those responsible for the public environment:

> If you have ever tried to negotiate a set of heavy swing doors and a steep flight of stairs with a pushchair and a small child; or needed to change a baby on a shopping trip; or had to wait an hour in a crowded waiting room with a bored toddler, you will understand the purpose of this book. Many people who are responsible for the design of the public environment, architects, planners, bank managers and shopkeepers etc lack this experience and fail to make adjustments or simple additions that could make life far easier and more enjoyable for children and their carers.

The authors seek to promote high-quality, accessible and welcoming facilities.

> In society today, women are disproportionately responsible for looking after children. We are concerned to avoid further

stereotyping of women and hope to encourage men to take an equal role, with higher status given to childcare in general. Children and their carers come from different backgrounds and cultures. It is not just parents who look after children, but many other people, such as other relatives, family friends, child-minders, nannies and au pairs. This book is intended to be relevant to the needs of all carers and children and within this framework it is necessary to state that we are opposed to any sexist, heterosexist, racist or able-bodied assumptions about childcare.

The book provides detailed advice, including specifications and architects' drawings. It covers pushchair access to buildings; public transport improvements (for example, specially designated child carriages on all long-distance trains, with play area, bed seats, etc.); provision of baby changing and feeding areas, and other facilities in shops, libraries, waiting rooms, swimming pools, etc.; and includes proposals for indoor and outdoor play equipment.[9]

ChildLine now provides a telephone-based source of advice and support for children, and many of their calls come from children who are being physically abused. Parents and other carers who feel under serious stress can call on local and national networks for advice and support – Parentline-Opus, the Parent Network, Parents Anonymous and others (see Appendix 2). But these organisations – always with limited funds and little official support – would acknowledge that much has to be done to ensure that all who need their services know about them, to encourage links and to reduce isolation.

Thus, while it is clear from the above survey that steps are being taken to make our society more child-centred and to help those who care for children, much, much more can be done. But we should not wait for this to happen before stopping the injustice of hitting children.

This book can only end as it began: hitting people is wrong – and children are people too. As the late Baroness Wootton said during an early and unsuccessful attempt to end school beating: 'If a thing is wrong today, it should be put right today, not tomorrow or the day after.'

# Appendix 1

## A CHRONOLOGY OF ATTEMPTS TO END THE LEGALISED HITTING OF CHILDREN

1669 Children's petition presented to Parliament – 'A modest remonstrance of that intolerable grievance our youth lie under, in the accustomed severities of the school discipline of this nation.'

1698 Revised version of petition appears as pamphlet aiming to persuade MPs to promote Bill to control use of school corporal punishment.

1783 Poland becomes first recorded country to abolish school beating; some others including Greece, Italy and Luxembourg appear never to have permitted it.

1820s Netherlands abolishes school beating.

1860 Chief Justice Cockburn held in *R*. v. *Hopley* (see page 99): 'By the law of England, a parent . . . may for the purpose of correcting what is evil in the child, inflict moderate and reasonable corporal punishment, always, however, with this condition, that it is moderate and reasonable.'

1861 Clarendon Commission report on nine 'public' schools says: 'Corporal punishment has . . . greatly diminished.'

1867 Belgium abolishes school beating.

1870 Austria abolishes school beating.

1872 Finland abolishes school beating.

1881 France abolishes school beating.

1889 Prevention of Cruelty to and Protection of Children Act passed – the first measure to limit maltreatment of children. Contains specific provision allowing physical punishment.
London schoolboys strike: one of four demands is an end to caning.

1905 Society for the Reform of School Discipline asks London County Council Education Committee to abolish; no success.

1906 Flogging in the British army is banned.

1917 Soviet Union abolishes school beating.

1923 Turkey abolishes school beating.

1930 Sub-area of local education authority bans beating in primary schools for 18 months; forced to reintroduce.

1933 Children and Young Persons Act consolidates legislation on cruelty to children, etc.; provision allowing parents, teachers and other carers to use physical punishment is re-enacted without debate.

1937 Joint National Union of Teachers/Association of Education Committees memorandum says: 'Corporal punishment is rapidly disappearing from public elementary schools.'

1938 Report of the Departmental Committee on Corporal Punishment (the Cadogan Committee) argues that 'the use of corporal punishment as a court penalty should be entirely abandoned', but the use of corporal punishment should be 'held in reserve as an ultimate sanction' for serious offences against prison discipline. Ministry of Education asks teacher unions what they feel about a change in the law; universal response is 'no change'.

1945 Committee Against Corporal Punishment in Schools formed with 50 MPs as members.

1947 A member raises the abolition of school corporal punishment in Parliament. Minister responds that National Foundation for Educational Research (NFER) will undertake inquiry.

1948 Birching as judicial punishment is abolished in the UK; remains in the Isle of Man.
     Rumania abolishes school beating.

1950 Portugal abolishes school beating.

1951 UK ratifies European Convenion on Human Rights; article 3 prohibits 'inhuman or degrading treatment or punishment'.

1952 NFER report finds 13 schools operating without physical punishment. Survey of teacher opinion shows 89.2 per cent agreeing that corporal punishment should be retained as last resort, 77.8 per cent 'strongly in favour' and just 3.5 per cent agreeing that it should be made illegal. Minister of Education says: 'Questions of school discipline are left to the discretion of local education and school authorities and I see no grounds for action on my part.'

1956 Ministry of Education memorandum insists that state schools must keep a punishment book to record instances of corporal punishment.

1957 Flogging in navy abolished.

1958 Sweden abolishes school beating.

1960 Report of Advisory Council on Treatment of Offenders, *Corporal Punishment*, advises strongly against its use in prisons.

1963 John and Elizabeth Newson publish first results of their longitudinal study of 700 Nottingham families. *Infant Care in an Urban Community* reveals that 62 per cent of mothers reported smacking their 1-year-old baby.

*Half our Future*, the 'Newsom' report on education of early leavers, says: 'We share the disquiet of those heads who feel that corporal punishment is likely to delay rather than to promote the growth of self-discipline and that it is humiliating to staff and pupils.'

1965 Research by J.W. Palmer on *Smoking, Caning and Delinquency* finds that a high proportion of children beaten for smoking actually increase their cigarette consumption at a time when smoking by children generally is in decline.

1966 Survey of teacher opinion by Plowden Committee shows 88.3 per cent still favouring corporal punishment 'as a last resort'. Sweden deletes provision allowing parental physical punishment from its family law.

1967 Cyprus, Denmark and Spain abolish school beating.

Corporal punishment in prisons and borstals abolished.

Plowden Report, *Children and their Primary Schools*, recommends abolition of corporal punishment in state and independent schools: 'We believe that the kind of relationship which ought to exist between teacher and child cannot be built up in an atmosphere in which the infliction of physical pain is regarded as a normal sanction.'

Revelations of beatings at Court Lees Approved School lead to inquiry and to a halving of the rate of use of the cane in approved schools (January–June 1967: 1,449 instances; July–December: 763).

Education Minister, Patrick Gordon Walker, says corporal punishment should disappear from schools; attempts to force ban on its use in special schools by issuing circular; forced to withdraw it by teacher unions.

1968 Cardiff Education Authority attempts to ban cane in primary schools for experimental period; opposition from local branches of teacher unions lead to reintroduction within two months.

STOPP (Society of Teachers Opposed to Physical Punishment) launched at public meeting.

*Four Years Old in an Urban Community* published: John and Elizabeth Newson's continuing research shows only 3 per cent of parents reporting that they do not smack their 4-year-olds, and only a quarter smacking less than once a week.

1969 In Finland, provision in criminal law stating that a petty assault is not punishable if committed by parents or others exercising lawful right to chastise child is deleted.

In UK, plans to abolish corporal punishment in approved schools dropped.

School pupil organisations hold protest marches in London: an end to caning is one of demands.

Liberal Party becomes first to declare opposition to school corporal punishment.

Education Committee of Inner London Teachers Association passes resolution supporting abolition in primary schools.

Ashley Bramall, leader of the Inner London Education Authority, announces intention to abolish in primary schools; launches consultation.

West Germany and some cantons of Switzerland abolish school beating.

1972 Norway removes provision allowing parents to use physical punishment from its criminal law.

1973 Inner London Education Authority abolishes cane in primary schools.

December 10:Second Reading of Baroness Wootton's Protection of Minors Bill to abolish school beating, defeated in House of Lords by 67 votes to 51.

One of the large voluntary child care organisations, National Children's Home, prohibits corporal punishment 'including every form of physical violence, or the infliction of physical pain'.

1974 National Children's Bureau's massive follow-up study of children born in a particular week of 1958 shows 80 per cent of 16-year-olds are in schools where corporal punishment is still used.

Survey in Edinburgh during two terms of 1973/74 shows over 10,000 instances of use of the 'tawse' (leather strap) on only 70,000 pupils.

1976 Dennis Canavan MP introduces abolitionist Bill; defeated in Commons by 180 votes to 120.

Mrs Grace Campbell and Mrs Jane Cosans apply to European Human Rights Commission in Strasbourg, alleging UK is in breach of Human Rights Convention because of use of school corporal punishment and lack of respect for parents' objections to it.

1977   Department of Education issues consultative letter on corporal punishment and holds meetings; teacher unions refuse to attend same meeting as STOPP and the National Union of School Students. Responses indicate 'a wide spectrum of opinion'.

1978   Handicapped and Deprived Children (Corporal Punishment) Bill to abolish corporal punishment for 'handicapped and deprived' children presented by Bruce Grocott MP; makes no progress due to opposition.

Trades Union Congress announces opposition to corporal punishment 'in principle'.

European Human Rights Court rules that judicial birching in the Isle of Man breaches Article 3 of Human Rights Convention which outlaws 'inhuman and degrading treatment or punishment'.

1979   International Year of the Child (IYC). Sweden becomes first country to add to its family law a specific prohibition on parents using physical punishment and other humiliating treatment of children.

Buckinghamshire celebrates IYC by reintroducing corporal punishment for infants.

A 14-year-old kills himself with a shotgun because he feared a school caning.

London Borough of Haringey becomes first education authority to abolish corporal punishment in all its maintained schools (this and other LEA-initiated bans do not apply to church schools).

1980   *Behind Closed Doors: Violence in the American Family* published: found 77 per cent of American parents believed slapping or spanking a 12-year-old was 'normal' and 71 per cent thought it 'good'.

Waltham Forest and Brent LEAs abolish school corporal punishment.

Labour Party conference votes for abolition of school corporal punishment.

During 1979/80, 1,985 slipperings are inflicted in four terms at Litherland High School, Sefton. Teacher Alan Corkish, who leaks details to STOPP, is later sacked.

1981   Children's Committee publishes 'issues paper' recommending to the government that 'The UK should embark on a progressive programme, governed by a specific timescale, to eliminate the use of corporal punishment on children and young people'; first official body to challenge parental as well as school corporal punishment.

In New Zealand, Jane and James Ritchie's book *Spare the Rod* is published, arguing for prohibition of all physical punishment of children.

Labour Party National Executive calls on all Labour-controlled LEAs to abolish school corporal punishment.

Public opinion poll results in Sweden show that between 1965 and 1981 the proportion of Swedish parents believing physical punishment is 'sometimes necessary' dropped from 53 to 26 per cent. The proportion believing that children should be raised without it increased from 35 to 71 per cent.

World's first government-appointed children's ombudsperson takes up office in Norway; one of her first tasks is to lobby for prohibition of parental physical punishment.

Inner London Education Authority, Derbyshire and Newham abolish school corporal punishment.

STOPP publishes *A Quarter of a Million Beatings*, an estimate of the total annual recorded beatings in English schools alone, based on analysis of statistics from punishment books in 10 LEAs.

1982 25 February: European Court of Human Rights finds UK guilty of breaching Convention by not respecting parental objections to corporal punishment; also guilty of denying Jeffrey Cosans his right to education; Jeffrey was suspended for refusing to be tawsed. After another case, *Mrs X* v. *UK*, is declared admissible by Human Rights Commission, Department of Education agrees as part of 'friendly settlement' to advise all LEAs that 'the use of corporal punishment may in certain circumstances amount to treatment contrary to Article 3'.

European Human Rights Commission reject application by Swedish parents alleging that Sweden's ban on parental physical punishment breached their right to respect for family life.

Nordic Council recommends that all five Nordic countries should ban parental physical punishment.

Teacher who caned a 12-year-old to 'bleeding point' for shoddy work is acquitted of assault.

National Union of Teachers annual conference overwhelmingly passes resolution declaring opposition to school beating.

George Younger, Secretary of State for Scotland, calls on Scottish LEAs to set themselves realistic target dates for abolition.

Circular from Church of England General Synod Board of Education calls on all Anglican schools to 'phase out and ultimately abolish the practice'.

Ireland abolishes school beating, leaving UK alone in Europe in maintaining it.

1983 UK forced by Human Rights Court to pay 'moral damages' of £3,000 to Jeffrey Cosans, also legal costs.

European Commission declares another case concerning school beating admissible.

National Association of Head Teachers, Secondary Heads Association, Ulster Teachers' Union and National Assocation of Welsh Teachers all adopt abolitionist policies.

Catholic Education Council calls on Catholic schools to phase out corporal punishment.

Council for Social Democracy (Social Democratic Party's policy-making body) calls for corporal punishment to be phased out over five years.

Department of Education issues consultative document, *Corporal Punishment in Schools*, on how to implement European Court judgment; proposes opt-out scheme.

STOPP publishes *Once Every Nineteen Seconds*, the title reflecting the society's 'conservative estimate' of the frequency of school beatings in England and Wales, based on punishment book statistics from 27 LEAs.

Finland joins Sweden in banning parental physical punishment.

1984 Teacher gets conditional discharge after punching a 15-year-old in the face and fracturing his cheekbone in three places.

STOPP publishes *Catalogue of Cruelty*.

STOPP survey of school prospectuses in 60 'beating' LEAs reveals that 94 per cent of boys secondary schools retain corporal punishment and 81 per cent of all secondary schools. Steven and Christopher Jarman, aged 15 and 14, are taken into care following prosecution of their mother for school non-attendance; the boys had been suspended from a Mid-Glamorgan school because, following a caning given to Christopher, their mother, Janice Jarman, refused to retract a written statement declaring her opposition to corporal punishment. Steven writes in *Childright*: 'I think it is very unfair that one man has been able to stop me and my brother from having education for 12 months, interfered with my life and split our family up – and that so many others have backed him up.'

Children's Legal Centre publishes results of survey of policies on physical punishment of children in care, finding 10 social services departments which have prohibited physical punishment of foster children.

1985 January: Education (Corporal Punishment) Bill presented to Commons; would give parents the right to opt their children out of school beating. Ridiculed by teachers, education organisations, etc.

Council of Europe Committee of Ministers, in report on action to combat family violence, recommend member states 'to review their legislation on the power to punish children in order to limit or indeed prohibit corporal punishment, even if violation does not necessarily entail a criminal penalty'.

Janice Jarman's appeal against conviction for her sons' non-school attendance is rejected and costs awarded against her. STOPP launches defence fund.

February: Children's Legal Centre magazine *Childright* publishes briefing on protecting children from parental physical punishment: 'Children and young people remain the only members of UK society not equally protected from assault.'

Survey of large representative sample of American families found 90 per cent of parents reported hitting 3-year-olds; about a third of 15- to 17-year-olds were hit in year of survey.

STOPP's education secretary, Tom Scott, is ordered to pay £6,000 libel damages and also costs estimated at £20,000; relying on official local authority report he alleged that an Essex headmistress had caned infants. In fact she had smacked them. Her libel case is backed by National Association of Head Teachers. Court refuses Scott permission to call expert witnesses; he is also forbidden to argue that there is no difference in principle between smacking and caning. Judge suggests it is an abuse of language to describe smacking as corporal punishment. (Later the verdict led to attempts, eventually abandoned, to declare Tom Scott bankrupt.)

July 4: House of Lords votes by 108 to 104 to turn Education (Corporal Punishment) Bill into abolitionist measure. Government withdraws Bill.

In Gillick case, Law Lords decide that parents' rights are recognised by law only as long as they are needed for the protection of the child; they yield to child's right to make decisions 'when he reached a sufficient understanding and intelligence to be capable of making up his own mind'.

1986 Denmark becomes third Nordic country to prohibit physical punishment by parents.

European Commission declares another case involving school beating admissible (more than 30 cases were under consideration in 1986 and 1987).

Criminal Injuries Compensation Board awards damages – an interim payment of £200 – to a boy injured by a teacher.

February 25: STOPP marks fourth anniversary of European Court ruling on *Campbell and Cosans* v. *UK* case by delivering an 'arrest warrant' to Mrs Thatcher at 10 Downing Street. Her crime – breaking European law by failing to implement the court's judgment.

April 17: During debate on new Education Bill, amendment to abolish corporal punishment is moved with all-party support in the Lords, and succeeds by majority of 2 (94 to 92).

Total of local authorities which have abolished school beating is now 34 out of 116 in England, Wales and Scotland; a further 7 have set date for abolition.

July 22: During the House of Commons report stage of the Education Bill, MPs vote for abolition by majority of 1 (231 to 230).

Children's Legal Centre holds London seminar on 'Protecting Children from Parental Physical Punishment'.

1987 August 15: Abolition of corporal punishment in all state-supported education takes effect in England, Wales, Scotland and Northern Ireland.

Edwina Currie, junior health minister, tells Parliament that physical punishment will be prohibited in all categories of children's home. Also says there are no circumstances in which corporal punishment would be appropriate in day nurseries or private nurseries.

Norway adds to its Parent and Child Act: 'The child shall not be exposed to physical violence or to treatment which can threaten his physical or mental health.'

Council of Europe Colloquy on 'Violence in the Family' recommends 'corporal punishment of children by their parents should be strongly discouraged. In some countries it is illegal, and efforts should be made to see whether it cannot be banned in other countries'.

1988 Report of judicial inquiry into child abuse in Cleveland prefaces its recommendations with: 'The child is a person not an object of concern.'

Professor Michael Freeman argues in *Childright* that the UK should follow the lead taken by Sweden, Finland, Denmark and Norway: 'If we are concerned to eliminate the evil of child abuse, we must ultimately accept that corporal punishment of children is child abuse'; article receives nation-wide publicity.

1989 January/February: During debates on Children Bill in House of Lords, amendment to remove 'endorsement' of parental physical punishment in the Children and Young Persons Act 1933 is discussed; no vote.

Amendment to Children Bill to prohibit foster parents hitting foster children is lost by 19 votes.

March: Austria prohibits physical punishment to children.

April: EPOCH – End Physical Punishment of Children is launched.

*Note: A shortened version of this chronology first appeared in* Childright, *no. 30 (September 1986).*

# Appendix 2

## BETTER WAYS OF CHILD-REARING: SOURCES OF HELP AND ADVICE FOR PARENTS

### Advice and Counselling in Emergency

For Parents

Chapter 6 refers to national networks of support groups for parents which can provide immediate advice and counselling:

*Parentline-OPUS*
106 Godstone Road, Whyteleafe, Surrey CR3 OGB. Tel: 01-645 0469
*Objects*: To prevent child abuse and maltreatment of infants and young children. Maintains a network of 30 self-help groups for parents under stress, running a befriending service, helplines, drop-in centres.

*Parent Network*
44–46 Caversham Road, London NW5 2DS. Tel: 01-485 8535
*Objects*: To help improve relationships and communication between parents and children by setting up national network of parent support groups; runs programmes to train parents as leaders to establish local groups.

*Parents Anonymous*
6–7 Manor Gardens, London N7 6LA. Tel: 01-236 8918
*Objects:* To offer friendship and help to those parents who are tempted to abuse their children and those who have done so; provides information service and meetings, telephone counselling and visiting service for parents, staffed by volunteer parents; nationwide network of groups.

## For Children

*ChildLine Charitable Trust*
Faraday Building, Queen Victoria Street, London EC4V 4BU. Tel:
01-236 2380. Freephone helpline: 0800-1111
*Objects*: To provide a free national helpline 'for children in trouble or
danger'.

*Children's Legal Centre*
20 Compton Terrace, London N1 2UN. Tel: 01-359 6251
*Objects*: Aims to promote recognition of children and young people
as individuals participating fully in all the decisions which affect their
lives; provides a free advice and information service for children and
adults by letter and phone (2 pm–5 pm weekdays), covering all
aspects of law and policy affecting children and young people in
England and Wales. Publications include leaflets, handbooks, reports
and a monthly magazine, *Childright*.

## Advice on Caring for Children

There is no shortage of written advice on child-rearing for parents
and other carers – look in any bookshop. But, unfortunately, quite a
few popular books still do not discourage the use of physical
punishment.

Two books which provide practical advice as well as a great deal of
encouragement to avoid physical punishment are:
*The Parents' A to Z : A Guide to Children's Health, Growth and
Happiness*, by Penelope Leach (Penguin Books, 1985; new edition,
1989). This substantial handbook has a major section on 'discipline,
self-discipline and learning how to behave'. It covers all ages from
birth to late adolescence, the various stages in learning how to
behave; common issues including obedience, lying, stealing, cheating,
and violence; common disciplinary techniques including 'arguing
and bargaining' and 'bribes and prizes'. It takes a very critical look at
physical punishments including hitting and confining children to
their room.
*Baby and Child: From Birth to Age Five*, by Penelope Leach (Penguin
Books, new edition 1989) – 'written from your baby or child's point of
view because, however fashion in child-rearing may shift and alter,
that viewpoint is both the most important and the most neglected'. It
is organised in approximate age-stages from birth up to 5, and a
comprehensive index guides the reader to a wealth of useful day-to-
day advice.

EPOCH – End Physical Punishment of Children (see page 175) publishes a booklet written by its parent education co-ordinator, Penelope Leach, *Smacking – a Short-cut to Nowhere*. Write to EPOCH, 77 Holloway Road, London N7 8JZ for details.

Some of the national child welfare organisations are increasing their involvement in parental education and producing leaflets, booklets, videos, etc. For details of these contact:

*National Society for the Prevention of Cruelty to Children*
67 Saffron Hill, London EC1N 8RS. Tel: 01-242 1626

*National Children's Home*
85 Highbury Park, London N5 1UD. Tel: 01-226 2033

*Barnardo's*
Tanners Lane, Barkingside, Ilford, Essex IG6 1QG. Tel: 01-550 8822

# Appendix 3

## MODEL BILL TO END PHYSICAL PUNISHMENT

### Children (Physical Punishment) Bill

A Bill to end the rights of parents and other carers to use physical punishment.

1 – (1)  Where, in any proceedings, it is shown that corporal punishment has been given to a child or young person by any person including a parent or guardian, giving the punishment cannot be justified on the ground that it was done in pursuance of a right exercisable by the person by virtue of his position as a parent or guardian or person having actual custody or control of the child or young person at the time.

(2)  Subject to subsection (3) below, references in this section to giving corporal punishment are references to doing anything for the purposes of punishing the child or young person concerned (whether or not there are also other reasons for doing it) which, apart from any justification, would constitute battery.

(3)  A person is not to be taken for the purposes of this section as giving corporal punishment by virtue of anything done for reasons that include averting an immediate danger of personal injury to, or an immediate danger to the property of, any person (including the child or young person concerned).

(4)  *A person does not commit an offence by reason of any conduct relating to a child or young person which would, apart from this section, be justified on the ground that it is done in pursuance of a right*

*exercisable by a parent or guardian or person having actual custody or control of a child or young person by virtue of his position as such.*

Schedule
Repeals

1.  In section 1 of the Children and Young Persons Act 1933 (cruelty to persons under sixteen) subsection (7) is hereby repealed.

*Notes: Similar changes would need to be made to the law in Scotland and Northern Ireland.*
*If subsection 4, printed in italics, is omitted, physical punishment becomes a criminal offence in addition to a civil wrong.*

# Appendix 4

**LEGISLATION PROHIBITING SCHOOL CORPORAL PUNISHMENT**

## Education (No. 2) Act 1986, Section 47

**47 Abolition of corporal punishment** (1) Where, in any proceedings, it is shown that corporal punishment has been given to a pupil by or on the authority of a member of the staff, giving the punishment cannot be justified on the ground that it was done in pursuance of a right exercisable by the member of the staff by virtue of his position as such.

(2)   Subject to subsection (3) below, references in this section to giving corporal punishment are references to doing anything for the purposes of punishing the pupil concerned (whether or not there are also other reasons for doing it) which, apart from any justification, would constitute battery.

(3)   A person is not to be taken for the purposes of this section as giving corporal punishment by virtue of anything done for reasons that include averting an immediate danger of personal injury to, or an immediate danger to the property of, any person (including the pupil concerned).

(4)   A person does not commit an offence by reason of any conduct relating to a pupil which would, apart from this section, be justified on the ground that it is done in pursuance of a right exercisable by a member of the staff by virtue of his position as such . . .

*Notes: Section 47 goes on to define 'pupil' and 'member of staff'.*
*Section 48 implements abolition for Scotland. The Education (Corporal Punishment) (Northern Ireland) Order 1987 implements abolition for Northern Ireland.*

# Notes

All titles of Scandinavian works published in their original language have been translated into English in the notes. Where a specific English translation exists this has been indicated.

## Introduction

1    Adrienne Rich, *Of Woman Born* (Virago, 1977), p. 280.
2    Education (No.2) Act 1986, section 47(3). See also the detailed explanation of law in Chapter 4.
3    Children Bill, as presented to Parliament, November 1988, parts III and IV.
4    Lloyd deMause (ed.), 'The evolution of childhood', in *The History of Childhood* (Souvenir Press, 1976), pp. 1–54.
5    Joav Merrick, 'Child Abuse and Neglect in Denmark: Epidemiological, Clinical and Social-Pediatric Aspects', thesis submitted to University of Copenhagen, 1988, para. 1.4.
6    Dean M. Herman, 'A statutory proposal to prohibit the infliction of violence upon children', *Family Law Quarterly*, vol. 19, no. 1 (Spring 1985).
7    Alice Miller, in particular: *For Your Own Good: The Roots of Violence in Child-Rearing*, and *The Drama of Being a Child* (Virago, 1987).
8    Alice Miller, *For Your Own Good*, pp. 11 and 56. These extracts from eighteenth-century German child-rearing manuals were originally published in Katharina Rutschky (ed.), *Schwarze Padagogik* (Berlin: Verlag Ullstein, 1978).
9    Samuel X. Radbill, 'A history of child abuse and infanticide', in R. E. Helfer and C. H. Kempe (eds), *The Battered Child* (Chicago: University of Chicago Press, 1974), p. 3.

10  *Corporal Punishment: An Issues Paper* (Children's Committee, 1981), p. 9.

11  Council of Ministers, Committee of Ministers, Recommendation no. R (85) 4: *Violence in the Family*, adopted 26 March 1985, Recommendation 12.

12  Michael Freeman, 'Time to stop hitting our children', *Childright*, no. 51 (October 1988), p. 5.

13  *Report of the Inquiry into Child Abuse in Cleveland 1987*, Cm 412 (HMSO, 1988), p. 245.

14  House of Lords, *Hansard*, debate on physical punishment of foster-children, 7 February 1989, cols 1443–53.

15  Convention on the Rights of the Child, text of draft adopted by working group of UN Commission on Human Rights, UN Commission of Human Rights ref. E/CN, 4/1989/29, 9 December 1988; italics added.

## 1   What's Wrong with Hitting Children?

1  European Commission of Human Rights, *Applications Nos 7511/76 and 7743/76, Grace Campbell and Jane Cosans against United Kingdom* (adopted 16 May 1980), p. 48.

2  Child Custody and Right of Access Act 1983, Finland, sections 1 and 4.

3  Parenthood and Guardianship Code, Sweden, as revised in 1983, chapter 6, section 1.

4  William J. Goode, 'Force and violence in the family', *Journal of Marriage and the Family*, vol. 33 (November 1971), p. 635.

5  Adah Maurer and James S. Wallerstein, *The Bible and the Rod* (End Violence Against the Next Generation, 977 Keeler Avenue, Berkeley, California 94708, USA, 1987), p. 7.

6  Lord Platt, House of Lords, *Hansard*, 10 December 1973, cols 904–5.

7  Jane and James Ritchie, *Spare the Rod* (Sydney, Australia: Allen & Unwin, 1981), p. 52.

8  Penelope Leach, *Baby and Child* (Penguin Books, 1979), p. 273. (A new fully revised edition is published by Penguin Books, 1989.)

9  Miriam Stoppard, *The Baby Care Book* (Dorling Kindersley, 1983), p. 253.

10  Thomas G. Power and M. Lynn Chapieski, 'Childrearing and impulse control in toddlers: a naturalistic investigation', *Developmental Psychology*, vol. 22, no. 2 (1986), pp. 271–5.

11    Quoted in Dean M. Herman, 'A statutory proposal to prohibit the infliction of violence upon children', *Family Law Quarterly*, vol. 19, no. 1 (Spring 1985).

12    Albert Bandura, *Aggression: A Social Learning Analysis* (Englewood Cliffs, NJ: Prentice-Hall, 1973), quoted in Herman, 'A statutory proposal', cit. at note 11.

13    John and Elizabeth Newson, *Four Years Old in an Urban Community* (Allen & Unwin, 1968), p. 428.

14    Norma D. Feshbach, 'The effects of violence in childhood', in David G. Gil (ed.), *Child Abuse and Violence* (New York: AMS Press Corp., 1979), p. 579.

15    Herman, 'A statutory proposal', cit. at note 11.

16    Series of studies reviewed by Birnbrauer, 'Generalization of punishment effects: a case study', *Journal of Applied Behaviour Analysis*, vol. 1 (1968), pp. 201, 203, 206.

17    Ritchie, *Spare the Rod*, p. 27.

18    Ibid., p. 30.

19    Bonnie E. Carlson, 'Children's beliefs about punishment', *American Journal of Orthopsychiatry*, vol. 56, no. 2 (April 1986), p. 308.

20    *Report of the Departmental Committee on Corporal Punishment*, Cmd. 5684 (HMSO, 1938).

21    *Corporal Punishment: Report of the Advisory Council on the Treatment of Offenders*, Cmnd. 1213 (HMSO, 1960), p. 27.

22    Peter Newell (ed.), *A Last Resort? Corporal Punishment in Schools* (Penguin Books, 1972), p. 77.

23    J. W. Palmer, 'Smoking, caning and delinquency in a secondary modern school', *British Journal of Preventive and Social Medicine*, vol. 19 (1965), p. 18.

24    David Reynolds, in M. Hammersley and P. Woods (eds), *The Process of Schooling* (Routledge & Kegan Paul, 1977). See also Michael Rutter and others, *Fifteen Thousand Hours* (Open Books, 1979).

25    David N. Jones, John Pickett, Margaret R. Oates and Peter Barbor, *Understanding Child Abuse* (Macmillan Education, 2nd edn 1987), p. 27.

26    Herman, 'A statutory proposal', cit. at note 11, p. 40.

27    Leach, *Baby and Child*, new edn 1989, p. 471.

28    Newson, *Four Years Old in an Urban Community*, p. 422; italics in original.

29    Ibid., p. 423.

30    Council of Ministers, Committee of Ministers, Recommenda-
      tion no. R (85) 4: *Violence in the Family*, adopted 26 March
      1985, Recommendation 12, pp. 7, 14.
31    US Surgeon General's Workshop on Violence and Public
      Health, 'Recommendations from the Workgroups', US Depart-
      ment of Health and Human Services, 1985.
32    *Inquiry into the Death of Lester Chapman: Report of an
      Independent Inquiry Commissioned by the County Councils and
      Area Health Authorities of Berkshire and Hampshire*, available
      from Archives Office, Shire Hall, Reading.
33    Audrey M. Berger, John F. Knutson, John G. Mehm and
      Kenneth A. Perkins, 'The self report of punitive childhood
      experiences of young adults and adolescents', *Child Abuse and
      Neglect*, vol. 7 (1988), pp. 251–62.
34    B. F. Steele and C. B. Pollock, 'A psychiatric study of parents
      who abuse infants and small children', in R. E. Helfer and C. H.
      Kempe (eds), *The Battered Child* (Chicago: University of
      Chicago Press, 1974), p. 89.
35    Åke Edfeldt, *Violence towards Children* (Stockholm: Akade-
      militteratur, 1979), p. 16.
36    Richard J. Gelles, Murray A. Straus and Suzanne K. Steinmetz,
      *Behind Closed Doors: Violence in the American Family* (New
      York: Anchor Press, 1980), p. 59.
37    Ritchie, *Spare the Rod*, p. 62.
38    J. A. Baldwin and J. E. Oliver, 'Epidemiology and family
      characteristics of severely abused children', *British Journal of
      Preventive and Social Medicine*, vol. 29 (1975), p. 217.
39    Teuvo Peltoniemi, 'Child abuse and physical punishment of
      children in Finland', *Child Abuse and Neglect*, vol. 7 (1983), pp.
      33–6.
40    A. Kadushin and J. A. Martin, *Child Abuse: An Interactional
      Event* (New York: Columbia University Press, 1981), p. 263.
41    Suzanne K. Steinmetz and Murray A. Straus (eds), 'Violent
      parents', in *Violence in the Family* (New York: Harper & Row,
      1974), p. 144; italics in original.
42    David G. Gil, 'A conceptual model of child abuse and its
      implications for social policy', in Steinmetz and Straus (eds),
      *Violence in the Family*, pp. 205, 206, 209.
43    Jones, Pickett, Oates and Barbor, *Understanding Child Abuse*,
      pp. 26–7.
44    Leach, *Baby and Child*, new edn 1989, p. 471.
45    Lesli Taylor and Adah Maurer, *Think Twice: The Medical*

*Effects of Physical Punishment* (End Violence Against the Next Generation, 1985; see note 5 above), p. 1.

46    J. E. Oliver and Ann Buchanan, 'Maltreatment of children as a cause of impaired intelligence', in Selwyn M. Smith (ed.), *The Maltreatment of Children* (MTP Press, 1978), p. 173.

47    Irwin A. Hyman, Wendy Zelikoff and Jacqueline Clarke, 'Psychological and physical abuse in the schools: a paradigm for understanding post-traumatic stress disorder in children and youth', *Journal of Traumatic Stress*, vol. 1, no. 2 (1988).

48    John L. Morris, Charles F. Johnson and Mark Clasen, 'To report or not to report: physicians' attitudes towards discipline and child abuse', *American Journal of Diseases of Children*, vol. 139 (February 1985), p. 194.

49    Edward R. Christophersen, 'The pediatrician and parental punishment', *Pediatrics* (Journal of the American Academy of Pediatrics), vol. 66, no. 4 (October 1980), p. 641.

50    John and Elizabeth Newson, *Infant Care in an Urban Community* (Allen & Unwin, 1965), p. 111.

51    Feshbach, 'The effects of violence in childhood', cit. at note 14, pp. 577, 578, 581; quotes A. Bandura and R. Walters, *Social Learning and Personality Development* (New York: Holt, Rinehart & Winston, 1963).

52    Association of Educational Psychologists: submission to Department of Education and Science consultation on school corporal punishment, 1977.

53    British Psychological Society, *Report of a Working Party on Corporal Punishment in Schools* (BPS, 1980).

54    G. C. Walters and J. E. Grusec, *Punishment* (San Francisco: W. H. Freeman, 1977).

55    Ritchie, *Spare the Rod*, pp. 52, 53.

56    R. E. Helfer, editorial, *Child Abuse and Neglect*, vol. 6, no. 2 (1982).

57    Robert R. Sears, Eleanor E. Maccoby and Harry Levin, 'The sources of aggression in the home' in Steinmetz and Straus (eds), *Violence in the Family*, p. 240.

58    Robert E. Larzelere, 'Moderate Spanking: Model or Deterrent of Children's Aggression in the Family?' Paper presented at Second National Conference on Family Violence, University of New Hampshire, USA, 1984.

59    Leach, *Baby and Child*, 1979 edn, p. 411.

60    Stoppard, *Baby Care Book*, p. 254.

61    Leonard B. Eron, L. Rowell Huesmann, Eric Dubow, Richard

Romanoff and Patty W. Yarmel, *Aggression and Its Correlates Over 22 Years* (Chicago: University of Illinois, 1983).

62    Leonard B. Eron, 'Parent–child interaction, television violence and aggression of children', *American Psychologist*, vol. 37, no. 2 (November 1982), p. 197.

63    Leopold Bellak and Maxine Antell, 'An inter-cultural study of aggressive behaviour on children's playgrounds', *American Journal of Orthopsychiatry*, vol. 44, no. 4 (July 1974).

64    Alice Miller, *For Your Own Good: The Roots of Violence in Child-Rearing* (Virago, 1987), pp. 65 et seq.

65    Gitta Sereny, *The Case of Mary Bell* (Arrow Books, 1974).

66    Gelles, Straus and Steinmetz, *Behind Closed Doors*, p. 74.

67    John and Elizabeth Newson, 'The Extent of Parental Physical Punishment in the UK'; italics in original. Paper prepared for Children's Legal Centre seminar on 'Protecting Children from Parental Physical Punishment', July 1986; available from authors, Child Development Research Unit, University of Nottingham, University Park, Nottingham, NG7 2RD.

68    Letter from Ralph S. Welsh to Dr Ludwig Lowenstein, July 1983; copy sent to author.

69    Ralph S. Welsh, 'Physical Punishment: Correction or Root of Delinquency and Other Problems', paper presented to 96th annual convention of American Psychological Association, August 1988. See also Ralph S. Welsh, 'Severe parental punishment and aggression: the link between corporal punishment and delinquency' in Irwin A. Hyman and James H. Wise (eds), *Corporal Punishment in American Education* (Philadelphia, Pa: Temple University Press, 1979).

70    Albert Bandura, *Relationship of Family Patterns to Child Behaviour Disorders*, Progress Report 1960, Stanford University, Project No. m – 1734, US Public Health Service, reported in Ritchie, *Spare the Rod*, p. 55.

71    'Violent juvenile delinquents: psychiatric, neurological, psychological and abuse factors', *Journal of the American Academy of Child Psychiatry*, vol. 18 (1979).

72    Studies quoted in Herman, 'A statutory proposal', cit. at note 11, p. 39.

73    Ibid., p. 28.

74    Murray A. Straus, 'Some social antecedents of physical punishment: a linkage theory interpretation', in Steinmetz and Straus (eds), *Violence in the Family*, p. 159. This is an abridged

version of paper, with same title, in *Journal of Marriage and the Family*, vol. 33 (November 1971), pp. 624–36.

75   Suzanne K. Steinmetz, 'Occupational environment in relation to physical punishment and dogmatism', in Steinmetz and Straus (eds), *Violence in the Family*, p. 166.

76   P. Brown and R. Elliot, 'Control of aggression in a nursery school class', *Journal of Experimental Child Psychology*, vol. 2 (1965), p. 103.

77   Feshbach, 'The effects of violence in childhood', cit. at note 14, p. 583.

78   S. J. Holmes and L. N. Robins, 'The influence of childhood disciplinary experiences on the development of alcoholism and depression', *Journal of Child Psychology and Psychiatry*, vol. 28, no. 3 (1987), p. 399.

79   Ian Gibson, *The English Vice: Beating, Sex and Shame in Victorian England and After* (Duckworth, 1978), p. 315.

80   Richard Krafft-Ebing, *Psychopathia Sexualis* (Stuttgart, 1886; translation by Harry E. Wedeck, under same title, New York: Putnam's, 1965); italics in original.

## 2   How Often Are Children Hit?

1    Åke Edfeldt, *Violence Towards Children* (Stockholm: Akademilitteratur, 1979), pp. 24, 25.

2    Valerie Yule, 'Why are parents tough on children?' *New Society*, 27 September 1985, p. 444.

3    John and Elizabeth Newson, 'The Extent of Parental Physical Punishment in the UK', paper presented to Children's Legal Centre seminar on 'Protecting Children from Parental Physical Punishment', July 1986. Unless otherwise stated, statistics and quotes from John and Elizabeth Newson in this chapter are taken from this paper. Copies available from authors, Child Development Research Unit, University of Nottingham, University Park, Nottingham NG7 2RD.

4    John and Elizabeth Newson, 'Parental punishment strategies with eleven-year-old children', in Neil Frude (ed.), *Psychological Approaches to Child Abuse* (Batsford, 1980), p. 73.

5    John and Elizabeth Newson, *Infant Care in an Urban Community* (Allen & Unwin, 1965).

6    Letter from John Newson to author, March 1989.

7    John and Elizabeth Newson, *Four Years Old in an Urban Community* (Allen & Unwin, 1968), p. 422; italics in original.

8    John and Elizabeth Newson, 'Parental punishment strategies', cit. at note 4, p. 72.

9    Urie Bronfenbrenner, 'Socialization and social class through time and space', in *Readings in Social Psychology* (New York: Holt, Rinehart & Winston, 1958).

10   Howard S. Erlanger, 'Social class differences in parents' use of physical punishment', in Suzanne K. Steinmetz and Murray A. Straus (eds), *Violence in the Family* (New York: Harper & Row, 1974), p. 150.

11   Murray A. Straus, 'Some social antecedents of physical punishment: a linkage theory interpretation' in Steinmetz and Straus (eds), *Violence in the Family*, p. 159. Abridged from article in *Journal of Marriage and the Family*, vol. 33 (1971), p. 658.

12   Suzanne K. Steinmetz, 'Occupational environment in relation to physical punishment and dogmatism' in Steinmetz and Straus (eds), *Violence in the Family*, p. 166; italics in original. The reference within the quote is to John L. Holland, 'Explorations of a theory of vocational choice: Part II, self description and vocational preference', *Vocational Guidance Quarterly* (Autumn 1963), p. 20.

13   Murray A. Straus and Richard J. Gelles, 'How violent are American families? Estimates from the national family violence re-survey and other studies', in Gerald T. Hotaling, David Finkelhor, John T. Kirkpatrick and Murray A. Straus (eds), *Family Abuse and Its Consequences* (Sage, 1988), p. 14.

14   Audrey M. Berger, John F. Knutson, John G. Mehm and Kenneth A. Perkins, 'The self-report of punitive childhood experiences of young adults and adolescents', *Child Abuse and Neglect*, vol. 12 (1988), p. 251.

15   Richard J. Gelles, Murray A. Straus and Suzanne K. Steinmetz, *Behind Closed Doors: Violence in the American Family* (New York: Anchor Press, 1980), p. 55.

16   Richard J. Gelles and Murray A. Straus, 'Societal change and change in family violence from 1975 to 1985 as revealed by two national surveys', *Journal of Marriage and the Family*, vol. 48 (August 1986), pp. 465–79.

17   Figures from End Violence Against the Next Generation, 977 Keeler Avenue, Berkeley, California 94708, USA.

18   Factsheet from National Coalition to Abolish Corporal

Punishment in Schools, 750 Brooksedge, Ste 107, Westerville, Ohio 43081, USA.

19    P. Amato, *Children in Australian Families: The Growth of Competence* (Sydney, Australia: Prentice-Hall, 1987).

20    *Community Attitudes Towards Domestic Violence in Australia*, Australian Government Office of the Status of Women, February 1988.

21    Jane and James Ritchie, *Spare the Rod* (Sydney, Australia: Allen & Unwin, 1981), pp. 25 et seq.

22    W. Havernick, *Schlage als Strafe* (1964), quoted in Dean M. Herman, 'A statutory proposal to prohibit the infliction of violence upon children', *Family Law Quarterly*, vol. 19, no. 1 (Spring 1985), p. 15.

23    Leopold Bellak and Maxine Antell, 'An intercultural study of aggressive behaviour on children's playgrounds', *American Journal of Orthopsychiatry*, vol. 44, no. 4 (July 1974), p. 509.

24    Anette Engfer and Klaus A. Schneewind, 'Causes and consequences of harsh parental punishment, an empirical investigation in a representative sample of 570 German families', *Child Abuse and Neglect*, vol. 6 (1982), pp. 129–39.

25    Letter from Anette Engfer to author, February 1989.

26    Herman, 'A statutory proposal', cit. at note 22, p. 16.

27    William J. Goode, 'Force and violence in the family', *Journal of Marriage and the Family*, vol. 33 (November 1971), p. 627.

28    Urie Bronfenbrenner, *Two Worlds of Childhood: US and USSR* (New York: Russell Sage Foundation, 1970).

29    Jill E. Korbin (ed.), *Child Abuse and Neglect: Cross-Cultural Perspectives* (Los Angeles: University of California Press, 1981).

30    David Levinson, 'Physical punishment of children and wife-beating in cross-cultural perspective', *Child Abuse and Neglect*, vol. 5 (1981), p. 193.

31    Herbert Barry and Lenora Paxon, 'Infancy and early childhood: cross-cultural codes', *Ethnology*, vol 2 (1971).

## 3  Banning Physical Punishment: The Scandinavian Experience

1     Letter to Children's Legal Centre from Edwina Currie, Parliamentary Under Secretary of State for Health, 29 February 1988.

2    Nordic Council Recommendation no. 10/1982/s, *Children and Their Environment*.

3    Council of Europe, Committee of Ministers, Recommendation no. R (85) 4: *Violence in the Family*, adopted 26 March 1985, Recommendation 12, p. 4.

4    Message from Bundesrat (Federal Council) to Bundesversammlung (Federal Assembly) on 'Modification of Swiss Civil Code (relations with Children)', 5 June 1974, ref. no. 323.31.

5    Message from Bundesrat concerning revision of Penal Code, 26 June 1985, ref. no. 213.5.

6    *Austria: National Report*, prepared for Council of Europe Colloquy on Violence within the Family: Measures in the Social Field, held in Strasbourg, 25–27 November 1987, p. 17.

7    *Denmark: National Report*, prepared for Council of Europe Colloquy, cit. at note 6, p. 10.

8    Letter to author from Lars Dencik, research director, Comparative Study of Childhood, Society and Development in the Nordic Countries, December 1988.

9    *Daily Mail*, 19 December 1988.

10   Interviewed during author's visit to Sweden, January 1989; also text of speech by Tor Sverne delivered to international audience, 1980.

11   SIFO, public opinion poll organisation, *Physical Punishment and Child Abuse*, report published April 1981, translated by Professor Adrienne Ahlgren Haeuser, University of Wisconsin, Milwaukee.

12   Swedish Children's Rights Commission, first report: *The Child's Right: 1 A Prohibition Against Beating*.

13   Parenthood and Guardianship Code; 1979 reform added to chapter 6, section 3, sub-para. 2. After the 1983 changes to the code, the prohibition on physical punishment is chapter 6, section 1.

14   Milk carton announcement was drafted by the organisation BRIS (Barnens Ratt I Samhallet) – Children's Rights in Society.

15   Pamphlet produced by Ministry of Justice, translated into minority languages including English: *Can You Bring Up Children Successfully without Smacking and Spanking?*

16   'Spank them don't Spoil them': audio-tape prepared for English-language lessons in Swedish secondary schools, translation included in Professor Adrienne Haeuser's report, *Reducing Violence Towards US Children: Transferring Positive*

*Innovations from Sweden* (1988) (University of Wisconsin, School of Social Welfare, PO Box 786, Milwaukee, Wisconsin 53201, USA), p. 65.

17   Bertil Ekdahl, Swedish Ministry of Justice, in *The Ombudsman and Child Maltreatment*, report of an international seminar organised by Rädda Barnen – Swedish Save the Children Federation, in Geneva, March 1980, p. 6.

18   Tor Sverne, text of speech to international audience, 1980.

19   European Commission of Human Rights, decision on admissibility of Application 8811/79: *Seven Individuals* v. *Sweden*, 13 May 1982.

20   BRIS (Barnens Ratt I Samhallet,) – Children's Rights in Society, Strindbergsg 32, 115 31 Stockholm.

21   For example, see *Daily Telegraph*, 15 August 1984: 'Father fined for spanking defiant son.'

22   Swedish Supreme Court decision, 5 December 1988, ref. B 990/87.

23   Information in letter from Tor Sverne to author, February 1989.

24   SIFO report published April 1981, cit. at note 11.

25   Klaus A. Ziegert, 'The Swedish prohibition of corporal punishment: a preliminary report', *Journal of Marriage and the Family* (November 1983) pp. 917–26.

26   Richard J. Gelles and Åke Edfeldt, 'Violence towards children in the United States and Sweden', *Child Abuse and Neglect*, vol. 10 (1986), p. 501.

27   Joan Senzek Solheim, 'A cross-cultural examination of the use of corporal punishment on children: a focus on Sweden and the United States', *Child Abuse and Neglect*, vol. 6 (1982), p. 147.

28   Adrienne Ahlgren Haeuser, 1981 Report – '1981 Swedish Bicentennial Fund Study Visit Report' (unpublished), School of Social Welfare, University of Wisconsin, Milwaukee; 1988 report, cit. at note 16.

29   National Child Environment Council (Barnmiljörådet), Box 22106, S – 10422 Stockholm. The council provides information and advice to help with child-proofing.

30   Statistics from Swedish Ministry of Social Affairs (Social-departement) and National Board of Health and Welfare (Socialstyrelsen).

31   Department of Health, *Children in Care of Local Authorities at 31 March 1986, England*, A/F 86/12.

32   Correspondence with Sirpa Utriainen, international officer,

Central Union for Child Welfare, Armfeltintie 1, 00150 Helsinki 15, Finland.

33 1969 amendment to Criminal Code repealed provision, ref. 21: 12.2, 827/48.

34 Two major new Acts covering child welfare were passed in 1983: Child Welfare Act and Child Custody and Right of Access Act. Translation available from Central Union for Child Welfare, address given at note 32.

35 Matti Savolainen, Ministry of Justice, Helsinki; interviewed 1989.

36 Ministry of Justice and National Board of Social Affairs, Helsinki; leaflet published 1984.

37 Central Union for Child Welfare (see note 32) in co-operation with National Boards of Health and Social Affairs – leaflets, stickers, posters. Kalle Justander, executive director of the Central Union, described the information campaign in 'Report of a child abuse awareness campaign', *Child Abuse and Neglect*, vol. 7 (1983), p. 485.

38 Teuvo Peltoniemi, 'Child abuse and physical punishment of children in Finland', *Child Abuse and Neglect*, vol. 7 (1983), p. 33.

39 Pekka Vuorista, *The Physical Punishment of Children Is Inherited*, quoted in Peltoniemi, 'Child abuse', cit. at note 38.

40 Maija and Martti Santasalo, *The Background of Child Battering*, Mannerheim League for Child Welfare, Publication no. B 36, Helsinki 1979 (Mannerheim League, 2, Linja 17, 00530 Helsinki).

41 Marja Korpilahti, *Child Battering in Finland and Sweden*, Research Institute of Legal Policy, Publication 50, Helsinki 1981.

42 Teuvo Peltoniemi, *Family Violence – Incidence and Attitudes in Finland 1981 and 1985*, A-Clinics Foundation, 1988 (A-Clinic Foundation, Fredrikinkatu 20A12, SF-00120 Helsinki).

43 Information from Heikki Sariola, research officer, Central Union for Child Welfare, Helsinki (see note 32).

44 Majority Act, section 2, para. 7.

45 Jorgen Graversen, 'Denmark: custody reform', *Journal of Family Law*, vol. 25, no. 1 (1986), p. 81.

46 *Denmark: National Report*, prepared for Council of Europe Colloquy on Violence within the Family: Measures in the Social Field, held in Strasbourg 25–27 November 1987.

47 Ole Varming, doctoral dissertation, 'Attitudes to Children',

Royal Danish School of Educational Studies, Copenhagen 1988.

48   Letter from Ole Varming to the author, February 1989.
49   M. Gregersen and A. Vesterby, 'Child abuse and neglect in Denmark: medico-legal aspects', *Child Abuse and Neglect*, vol. 8 (1984), p. 83.
50   *Denmark: National Report*, see note 46.
51   Joav Merrick, 'Child Abuse and Neglect in Denmark: Epidemiological, Clinical and Social-Pediatric Aspects', thesis submitted to University of Copenhagen, November 1988; also 'Physical punishment of children in Denmark: an historical perspective', *Child Abuse and Neglect*, vol. 10 (1986), p. 263.
52   *Northern Echo*, 16 January 1987: 'Watch it, parents'.
53   Information from Målfrid Grude Flekkoy, Norwegian Children's Ombudsperson (Barneombudet), interviewed by author January 1989; Barneombudet, Postboks 8004 Dep, 0030 Oslo 1.
54   Norway Official Report, *Child Abuse and Neglect*, NOU 1982:26.
55   Norwegian Ministry of Justice proposal, 17 October 1986.
56   Official reports of debates in Norwegian Parliament: Odelstinget, 15 January 1987; Lagtinget, 22 January 1987.
57   People's Movement for Children (Folkeaksjonen for Barn), Arbinsgt. 1, 0253 Oslo 1.
58   Letter from Turid Vogt Grinde, Norwegian Institute of Child Welfare Research, to author, December 1988.

## 4   The Law and Physical Punishment in the UK

1    *Parliamentary Debates*, 3rd series (1889), vol. 337, cols 1379–86.
2    *Parliamentary Debates*, 3rd series (1889), vol. 338, col. 956.
3    Halsbury, *Laws of England* (Butterworths), para. 1216, p. 647.
4    Bromley, *Family Law* (Butterworths, 6th edn 1981), p. 110. Quoting Blackstone's *Commentaries*, p. 445.
5    *R*. v. *Jackson* (1891) 1 QB 671.
6    Hale, *Pleas of the Crown*, vol. 1, pp. 31, 261.
7    *R*. v. *Hopley* (1860) 2 F & F 202.
8    *R*. v. *Griffin* (1869) 11 Cox CC 402.
9    *Ryan* v. *Fildes* (1938) 3 All ER 517, 520.
10   Case referred to in David N. Jones, John Pickett, Margaret R.

Oates and Peter Barbor, *Understanding Child Abuse* (Macmillan Education, 2nd edn 1987), p. 87.

11   Cases reported in *STOPP News*, vol. 2, no. 1 (January 1986).

12   Gillick case: High Court: (1984) 1 All ER 365; Court of Appeal: (1985) 1 All ER 533; House of Lords: (1985) 3 All ER 402.

13   Stephen Sedley, QC, 'Child welfare limits parents' rights to punish or restrain', *Childright*, no. 26 (April 1986), p. 18.

14   John Eekelaar, 'Gillick: further limits on parents' right to punish', *Childright*, no. 28 (June 1986), p. 9.

15   See, in particular, 'recommendations' on children, *Report of the Inquiry into Child Abuse in Cleveland 1987*, Cm 412 (HMSO, 1988), p. 245. Official guidance: Home Office Circular: *The Investigation of Child Sexual Abuse*, HO Circular 52/1988; *Diagnosis of Child Sexual Abuse: Guidance for Doctors*, DHSS (HMSO, 1988).

16   Michael Freeman, 'Time to stop hitting our children', *Childright* no. 51 (October 1988), p. 5.

17   Children Bill as presented to Parliament, November 1988, parts III and IV.

18   House of Lords, *Hansard*, 23 January 1988, col. 548.

19   Unpublished legal opinion from Stephen Sedley, QC, obtained by Children's Legal Centre, February 1989.

20   House of Lords, *Hansard*, 16 February 1989, cols 346, 350–1.

21   House of Lords, *Hansard*, 16 March 1989, cols 407–10.

22   Written answer, House of Commons, *Hansard*, 9 March 1987, cols 64–6.

23   Residential Care Homes (Amendment) Regulations 1988, SI 1988/1192 (HMSO).

24   See note 22.

25   'Is hitting caring?' *Childright*, no. 4 (February 1984), p. 8.

26   For example, Quebec Child and Family Services Act 1984, section 97: 'No service provider or foster parent shall inflict corporal punishment on a child or permit corporal punishment to be inflicted on a child . . .'

27   'Revised data on corporal punishment', from US Children's Bureau, quoted in *The Last? Resort*, vol. 16, no. 1 (Fall 1987), newsletter of the Committee to End Violence Against the Next Generation (EVAN-G), 977 Keeler Avenue, Berkeley, California 94708, USA.

28   Children's Legal Centre submission to Department of Health and Social Security consultation; reported in *Childright*, no. 46 (April 1988), p. 8.

29    House of Lords, *Hansard*, 7 February 1989, col. 1452.


**5  The Long Struggle to End School Beating in the UK**

1     C. B. Freeman, 'The children's petition of 1669 and its sequel', *British Journal of Educational Studies*, vol. 14 (May 1966), p. 216.

2     European Court of Human Rights Judgment: *Campbell and Cosans* v. *UK*, Strasbourg, 25 February 1982.

3     European Commission of Human Rights, Applications nos. 7511/76 and 7743/76, *Campbell and Cosans* v. *UK*, Report adopted 16 May 1980, Strasbourg.

4     European Commission of Human Rights, *Mrs X* v. *UK*, Report adopted 17 December 1981; Department of Education and Science circular letter to local education authorities, 5 March 1982.

5     European Commission of Human Rights, Application no. 9471/81, *Mrs X and Miss X* v. *UK*, Report adopted 18 July 1986, Strasbourg.

6     STOPP Press Notice, 'Corporal Punishment in Private Schools, Results of Survey', 16 May 1988.

7     Peter Newell (ed.) *A Last Resort? Corporal Punishment in Schools* (Penguin Books, 1972), gives details of the early history of the campaign.

8     British Psychological Society, *Report of a Working Party on Corporal Punishment in Schools* (BSP, 1980).

9     STOPP, *A Quarter of a Million Beatings: An Analysis of Official Statistics Exposing the Myth that Corporal Punishment Is Rarely Used*, July 1981 (STOPP publications are no longer available).

10    STOPP, *Once Every Nineteen Seconds*, 1983 (see note 9).

11    Leila Berg, *Risinghill: Death of a Comprehensive* (Penguin Books, 1968).

12    Peter Newell,'The beaters beaten', *Times Educational Supplement*, 14 August 1987.

13    'Caning company sold to Dai Llewellyn', *Daily Telegraph*, 1 August 1986.

14    *Daily Mail*, 25 June 1984.

15    Letter to STOPP education secretary from Department of Education and Science, Schools 2 branch official, 23 November 1981.

16    House of Commons, *Hansard*, 28 January 1985, col. 42.

17    Children's Legal Centre briefing, 'Education (Corporal Punishment) Bill – unworkable and unjust', *Childright*, no. 15 (March 1985), summarises criticisms of the Bill.
18    House of Lords, *Hansard*, 4 July 1985, cols 1314, 1324, 1332.
19    House of Lords, *Hansard*, 17 April 1986, cols 788–801.
20    Children's Legal Centre briefing, *Government Plans for Corporal Punishment: Unworkable, Unjust – and Still in Breach of Human Rights Code*, July 1986.
21    Case reported in *STOPP News*, vol. 2, no. 6 (Summer 1987), p. 4.
22    House of Commons, *Hansard*, 22 July 1986, cols 226–78.
23    Abolition took effect on 15 August 1987, when section 47 (England and Wales) and section 48 (Scotland) of the Education (No. 2) Act 1986 and the Education (Corporal Punishment) (Northern Ireland) Order 1987 were implemented.

## 6   What Can Be Done Now: Next Steps in the UK

1    Jane and James Ritchie, *Spare the Rod* (Sydney, Australia: Allen & Unwin, 1981).
2    B. A. Carson, *Advice on Childrearing Manuals on the Use of Physical Punishment*, Family Research Laboratory, University of New Hampshire, USA, 1987.
3    National Society for the Prevention of Cruelty to Children, parents' booklet, *Putting Children First*, 1989. Available from NSPCC, 67 Saffron Hill, London EC1N 8RS.
4    National Children's Home, Children in Danger Campaign, *You and Your Children 4: Tips for Young Parents*. Available from NCH, 85 Highbury Park, London N5 1UD.
5    Johnson Foundation, press release: 'National Group Adopts Statement Opposing Parental Use of Physical Punishment on Children', 24 February 1989; Johnson Foundation, PO Box 547, Racine, Wisconsin 53401–0547, USA.
6    Adrienne Rich, *Of Woman Born: Motherhood as Experience and Institution* (Virago, 1977), p. 279.
7    John and Elizabeth Newson, *Infant Care in an Urban Community* (Allen & Unwin, 1965), pp. 113–14.
8    We Welcome Small Children – National Campaign, Newsletter No 6, Spring 1988; details of membership, etc. from: 93 Belsize Lane, London NW3 5AY.
9    *Thinking of Small Children: Access, Provision and Play*,

published by We Welcome Small Children Campaign, Women's
Design Service and London Borough of Camden, March 1988.

# Index

# EPOCH

End Physical Punishment
of Children

**Hitting people is wrong – and children are people too**
This new national organisation aims to end the physical
punishment of children by parents and other carers. It was
launched in April 1989, with Peter Newell as its co-ordinator,
and Penelope Leach as parent education co-ordinator.
EPOCH hopes to achieve its aim through public education, information,
research and campaigning for legal reforms.

First and foremost, EPOCH wants to see changes in
attitudes to children; to see children recognised as people –
and recognition that it is as wrong to hurt a child as it is to
hurt another adult. Far from having a right or even a duty to
hit children, parents have a right to information about non-
violent ways of bringing up their children, and a duty to
discipline them with their heads and hearts rather than with
their hands or implements.

The law protects the rest of us from violence at the hands
of anyone else. Why shouldn't it protect children too?

You can become a supporter of EPOCH by sending a
minimum donation of £12 (£6 for unwaged people) to:
EPOCH, 77 Holloway Road, London N7 8JZ.

As a supporter you will receive regular information on the
issue. If you want further details, please send a stamped
addressed envelope to the above address.

Other titles in the **Society Today** series:

Walter Schwarz
*The New Dissenters: The Nonconformist Conscience in the Age of Thatcher*

Colin Ward
*Welcome, Thinner City: Urban Survival in the 1990s*
(September 1989)

John Withington
*Shutdown: The Anatomy of a Shipyard Closure*

*For further details, please write to the sales manager, Bedford Square Press, 26 Bedford Square, London WC1B 3HU.*